KILLERS ON MULHOLLAND DRIVE

Ronald E Bowers

Former Senior Prosecutor
Los Angeles County District Attorney's Office

Some names and locations have been changed to protect the privacy of individuals connected with these cases. Certain events and statements have been inferred from the facts of these cases as well as from public articles about these cases.

Ronald E. Bowers, Publisher
losangelestruecrime@aol.com

ISBN 978 -1-7326655-3-8

First release July 2015

Second release June 2017

INTRODUCTION

How and why are the names of certain streets and roads well known by people all around the world? When someone hears the word Appian Way, one immediately thinks of an ancient road in Rome. Likewise when the name Champs Elysees is mentioned, of course we envision a wide boulevard in Paris. These highways are recognized because of the historic significance attached to them. Other roads become known for other reasons. People have become familiar with street names like Mulholland Drive, Sunset Boulevard, Rodeo Drive, Melrose Place, and Pacific Coast Highway all are somehow connected to the entertainment business involving movies and television.

'Mulholland Drive' is one of those roads that have worldwide recognition. It has gained fame mostly because of all the Celebrities who claim it to be their home address. What makes it so desirable is the spectacular views of the city lights at night. It offers a panorama view of Hollywood below and allows one to gaze out over the city of Los Angeles which seems to extend as far as the eye can see.

Besides the incredible views, Mulholland Drive stretches some 22 miles dividing the second largest city into two parts described as Downtown Los Angeles and the other being the San Fernando Valley. Not too many streets and highways have gained the status of having a movie named after them. The movie titled *Mulholland Drive* may have given people the impression that this road was some type of grand highway, like Rodeo Drive, with its glitz and glamour. However, the real Mulholland Drive is mostly a narrow two-lane rural road that runs across the ridge of the Santa Monica Mountains. It consists of an unimpressive asphalt road with a patchwork of filled potholes. Overtime this section of highway has played host to murder, robbery, rape, and some scandalous crimes.

Since I am a native of the Los Angeles area, I am well aware how most Angelinos became familiar with Mulholland Drive. When I attended UCLA, it was well known that a way to impress a date was driving up to Mulholland and find a turnout to take in the spectacular views. It was informally known as a Lover's Lane offering a romantic setting where one felt protected from being disturbed by obtrusive police officers. In retrospect, a little smooching on Mulholland Drive may not have been the wisest decision a young couple could take part in.

However, as I matured and worked for the DA's Office I acquired a different prospective of Mulholland Drive. I became exposed to an endless number of crime reports of robberies and rapes. I learned over the years how such a beautiful place can turn deadly as night falls. As time progressed, the crimes seemed to become more violent with more resulting in murder. When I contemplated writing this book about Mulholland Drive so many cases came to mind. I realized that you, the reader, don't have the time nor interest in hearing about every crime I have seen involving this highway. After reviewing dozens of cases, I decided to include several cases that best demonstrate the true nature of Mulholland Drive.

The first case to be discussed is one of the saddest which involves the life of such a promising individual. That was the unfortunate death of Ennis Cosby who was shot in an attempted 'robbery gone bad'. Without any doubt, he embodied everything good that a parent could want in a son. The case actually occurred on Skirball Center Drive only a short distance from Mulholland Drive and the 405 Freeway. As painful as it is to discuss such a sad depressing case, there is a story that needs to be told. The defendant's main focus was on robbing people to get money to buy drugs. It just so happened, that Ennis Cosby was in the wrong place at the wrong time, which was no fault of his own.

What makes this case so compelling is the fact that the defendant almost got away with murder. If it were not for the incredible jobs done by the LAPD and the prosecutor, Anne Ingalls, this defendant would have continued to victimize the public and possibly causing more innocent lives being lost. My involvement occurred during the pretrial stages and continued up until the Argument. This was a case in which the trial strategy played a fundamental role in the outcome of the case.

This book reviews cases that happened on or near Mulholland Drive starting with the 405 Freeway where the Cosby case occurred and continuing east to the intersection of Beverly Glenn Boulevard. This is a heavily used road the inhabitants use to cross the mountain range. One of the places on the road is the location where the Manson family drove up to Mulholland after the infamous Sharon Tate murders. Tex Watson got out of the car and threw away the revolver he used to shoot several of the victims. Later, after disposing of some of their bloody clothing, they proceeded down the hillside to return to the Span Ranch where the Manson family resided. Needless to say, when the gun was recovered, many or the residents of Mulholland Drive were terrified to learn that the Manson Family was roaming around in their area.

In that same general area, the Menendez Brothers disposed of the two Mossberg shotguns used to kill their parents by throwing them over the side of Mulholland Drive. After they had shot and killed their parents, Lyle Menendez with his bother Erik, quickly left their home in Beverly Hills proceeded up Beverly Glen to the crest of the mountains. In order to get rid of the most incriminating evidence, the shotguns, they tossed them into the deep ravines. Even to this day neither shotgun has been found attesting to the fact of what a desolate area this is even though it is located on the top of a giant metropolis.

To continue our journey eastward on Mulholland Drive, we weave pass a number of incredible towering homes with their infinity pools surrounded by home entertainment centers. Architects have been given blank checks to design the biggest and the most glamorous house in order for their owners to impress all their neighbors. About half way across the mountain drive, one comes to a bend named 'Bad Boys Curve' where a private driveway is closed off by an iron gate. There are no markings as to who lives behind this sturdy gate. No signs, no names provide any suggestion as to whose residence lies tucked away on the hilltop.

Only the Hollywood insiders know this was the entrance to Marlon Brandon's estate. He shares the driveway with Jack Nicholson, his neighbor. It may seem strange that these two well-known actors, who were leading men in their own day, shared a joint entry gate to their hillside homes. The next case we will be reviewing is the infamous Christian Brando case in which he was accused of murdering his sister's boyfriend in Marlon Brando's house. This case created a real dilemma for both sides. Much has been written about it but few have known the inside facts as to the problems both sides were confronted with. Many of the pundits have spun stories around this case, but it is time that the true facts are discussed.

I try to set the record straight since the dust has settled and some of the reputations need not be jealously guarded any longer. On one of my visits to Tahiti, I went to the cemetery where Cheyenne Brando and her finance Dag Drollet are buried in the Drollet family plot. I have spoken to the natives to learn what is happening to Marlon's atoll which has been carefully developed into the exclusive Brando Hotel.

Even after Brando's death, he still has a profound effect on Tahiti, his beloved paradise.

After leaving the Christian Brando crime scene, we proceed next door to visit the site of the longest continuing case in the history of the Los Angeles County Superior Court. Although it didn't comprise of a murder, it received more attention than most homicide cases. It involved a child sexual molestation case which, by its very nature, wouldn't generate much notice except for the fact that the suspect was a well-known individual. That suspect was none other than America's most sympathetic character, Roman Polanski, since his wife, Sharon Tate, had been brutally murdered by the Manson family. His baby had been hacked to death by a knife wielding Susan Atkins.

The Hollywood establishment had commiserated with the tragedy that Roman Polanski had endured. Luckily, he was away in Europe when the massacre occurred. Otherwise, he would have been 'pushing up daisies' like his wife and child. I wasn't originally involved in the prosecution of the Polanski case since the case was handled by prosecutor Roger Gunson. I was aware of all the problems with the prosecution of the case and remembered the relief when the case was settled by a plea bargain which required Polanski to serve 90 days in a State Prison Diagnostic Program. During my career, I had settled dozens of cases by sending defendants to this Program. I knew it was a great therapeutic way of getting a suspect's attention as to the error of his ways. For 90 days, the defendant would hear the loud clanging of the prison doors closing behind him. The normal person with an IQ above 80 would realize that he didn't want to spend the next 5 to 10 years behind bars.

The end result was that after 90 days in custody, the defendant was eager to agree to any terms of probation as long as he didn't have to return to state prison. In

Roman Polanski's case, he served only **47 days** in confinement and was released early for some unknown reason. This incensed the judge and Polanski got the word he might be headed for a lengthy prison sentence. He decided to leave town without waiting to see what sentence the judge would impose. He flew to France so he couldn't be extradited. For years he remained on the lamb becoming America's number one 'Fugitive.'

In the early "90's", one of my many duties was overseeing the DA's Extradition Unit. That was when I became involved in tracking down Roman Polanski and bringing him back for sentencing in the Child Sexual Molestation case. It became a 'Cat and Mouse Game' of trying to catch him while he was visiting another country. One day I got lucky and learned he was being honored in Canada as one of the great film directors of all times. The Toronto Film Festival was giving him a prestigious award.

I alerted the Canadian Mounties and asked them to take Polanski into custody as soon as he stepped off the plane. All precautions were taken so that there was no way Polanski would slip through the cracks without being snared by red coated Mounties. I was certain that this time I would be the one to claim to have caught 'The Fugitive.' To my surprise, someone had tipped off Polanski and he never got on the flight in Paris headed to Toronto. The next day I tried to recap what went wrong. I couldn't prove who leaked the information to him. All I could say was that the mouse had outsmarted the cat one more time. I tried to apprehend him but I wasn't successful in bringing him to justice.

In order not to dwell on the lack of success in the Polanski case, our story continues down Mulholland Drive close to its eastern end. Here again, I worked on another sad case like the Ennis Cosby case. It involved another 'Robbery gone bad,' but with a twist as to how the human spirit can overcome all obstacles. It was a typical robbery on Lover's Lane. It could have happened to any young person growing up in Los Angeles who decided to take a date up to Mulholland Drive to enjoy the city lights.

Little did the young man realize that a group of robbers would come up to his driver's window and point a gun at him. He had to make a split-second decision as to how to react. Should he run or stay to be robbed. This was the most important choice he would ever make in his life. I remember preparing this case for trial and thinking that this could have been me or any of my friends when we were younger. Although this case received little or no attention by the news media, it demonstrated the strength of human perseverance. Also, it showed how law enforcement through the LAPD dispatchers and a helicopter pilot worked together as a team to safe a young woman's life.

Mulholland Drive is a road that has so many stories to tell. Most of them are regarding the celebrities whose homes are squeezed together along the road. But there are the human tragedies that have occurred there that have created the allure and mystic known as Mulholland Drive. If this road could speak, it would have so many tales to tell. Mulholland Drive is more than a name. It is more than a road covered by asphalt. These four cases illustrate that the road has a life of its own. At times it is a road full of joy and dazzling views while at other times, it is a road paved with pain and sorrow.

CONTENTS

Shooting of Ennis Cosby

People vs. Mikhail Markhasev

CHAPTER 1 ENNIS COSBY HAS A FLAT TIRE

Is students we were required to read the ***Tale of Two Cities*** by Charles Dickens that he wrote in1859 which began as follows:

"It was the best of times, it was the worst of times, it was the age of wisdom, it was the age of foolishness, it was the epoch of belief, it was the epoch of incredulity, it was the season of Light, it was the season of Darkness, it was the spring of hope, it was the winter of despair, we had everything before us, we had nothing before us, we were all going direct to Heaven, we were all going direct the other way..."

This describes the story you are about to read. Ennis Cosby, on January 16, 1997, was enjoying his winter break from studying for his PhD from Columbia University Teachers College in New York. The very next day he was returning to New York to resume his studies. Earlier in the evening he had played basketball with a group of friends. To cap off the evening, he was going to meet with a rather fascinating lady named Stephanie C (Pseudonym) who was 47 years old, a screenwriter who lived in Sherman Oaks.

Ennis's father had made America laugh for years but Ennis shied away from the entertainment industry and felt an urge to help young people with learning disabilities. His father had drummed into him the importance of education and early on he had the opportunity to work with young children with 'Special Needs' and he gained an immense satisfaction seeing them advance through learning.

Unquestionably, it was the best of times for Ennis because of his parent's financial position, he was able to comfortably pursue what he was interested in. During this winter break, he had the opportunity to stay in one of his parent's homes located on the edge of Brentwood. Although his parents primarily called their Connecticut/ Pennsylvania estate their main abode, but when the winter set in, Ennis and his parents enjoyed the warmer climate on the west coast. His parent's Tudor style home almost across the street from Steven Spielberg's sprawling estate, was nestled in one of the most pleasant and safest places in the 'City of the Angles.' The Rich and Famous have homes sprinkled throughout the rolling hills with their spectacular views of the Pacific Ocean.

Just over the hill from their house was the Will Roger's historic house with the adjacent plush green polo field. It seemed ironic that Will Roger's and Ennis's dad, Bill Cosby, had both been given the title as 'America's Humorist.' Will Rogers in 1928 made famous the following line, "I don't make jokes. I just watch the government and report the facts." Some people might think those words are still true today. Rogers most noted quote was, "When I die, my epitaph...is going to read, 'I joked about every prominent man of my time, but I never met a man I didn't like.' I am so proud of that, I can hardly wait to die so it can be carved." Unfortunately, this came true all too soon when he and his friend aviator, Willy Post, crashed their small plane in Alaska killing both of them.

Bill Cosby, as a comedian, had numerous quotes such as, "Parents are not interested in justice, they're interested in peace and quiet;" "When you become senile, you won't know it;" "Man can not live by bread alone, he must have peanut butter;" "Women don't want to hear what you think. Women want to hear what they think- in a deeper voice;" "Every closed eye is not sleeping, and every open eye is not seeing." Bill Cosby, as a comedian, had a message to all races and wasn't afraid to declare that education paved the way to success even though some groups wanted success handed to them.

On this January evening in 1997, Ennis wasn't thinking of anything profound but looking forward to talking to Stephanie C, an aspiring screenwriter, who he had met a week earlier at another social function.

Although she was older at the age of 47 and he was 27 years old, they had much in common in that she was born into an entertainment family since her father had been one of the producers of the Honeymooner's TV series starring Jacky Gleason. Both Ennis and Stephanie had an intensive conversation about relationships that ended in heartache. Ennis had just recently broken up with a longtime girlfriend. What knowledge that Stephanie was able to contribute to the conversation was that she had been happily (so to say) married six times. This seemed to qualify her as an expert in relationships.

On the night in question, he called her and she had just gotten in from a date and she invited him to come over to her place so the two could talk. Earlier in the evening he had a friendly basketball game, after which Ennis returned home and quickly showered, cleaned up, and within a half hour he was grabbing the keys to the family's Mercedes sports convertible. He used it since his folks weren't in town. He backed it out of the garage and as he pulled out of the driveway he reached over to the radio trying to find a music station. Possibly he heard ***I Believe in You and Me*** by Whitney Houston which sort of set the tone for the evening. As the Mercedes maneuvered down the street, the next tune could have been ***Un-Break My Heart*** by Toni Braxton. Ennis had to smile to himself about his recent romance which seemed to have hit rough water when he decided to pursue his Ph.D.

The music inspired Ennis to believe that maybe Stephanie C could give him some pointers as to experiencing "It was the best of times." He realized that Stephanie lived in Sherman Oaks which is in the San Fernando Valley. Since the Cosby's lived in Brentwood, Ennis knew that he would have to take the 405 Freeway to reach her place. Geographically the Santa Monica mountain range divides the City of Los Angeles into two cities. The Central Los Angeles section is massive and reaches all the way down to San Pedro while the San Fernando Valley consists of a vast basin, surrounded by mountain ranges on all sides. The two cities are connected by the 405 freeway on the West side and the Cahuenga Pass (the old 101 Freeway) on the East side.

Although, during rush hour Ennis would never have attempted to go to Stephanie's place. For Angelinos the 405 is known as the 'slow moving parking lot.' This freeway is the main artery between the two cities. The state Caltran Division is continually widening the freeway but no matter how wide they make it, it can't absorb the thousands of cars during Rush Hour. However, Ennis wasn't concerned with crossing over the 405, since it was late and it wouldn't be crowded.

At the Sunset on ramp to the 405 Freeway, Ennis made his turn going up the hill. He gunned the sports car and could feel the power of the engine propel him to maneuver around several slower cars on the right. At that moment in time, the world couldn't be better for Ennis Cosby. No doubt Ennis was experiencing the 'Best of

Times' until he heard a thumping sound coming from the left front of the car. He eased off of the accelerator and felt a vibration that seemed to be shaking the car. He glanced in his right-hand mirror to see if he could move over in traffic. Other cars around him jockeyed out of his way to the right-hand lane.

His brain was trying to process all this noise and vibration. Could it be a flat tire? The car was relatively new and had been kept in excellent mechanical condition. Now Ennis was experiencing difficulty in turning the steering wheel. His main concerned was trying to get off the freeway in one piece. The sign in front said 'Skirball Center' turn off. He was traveling all of five miles an hour and it seemed to take forever to reach the off ramp. Then he was faced with a traffic signal and had to make an immediate decision whether to turn right or left. He glanced to the left and could see there was room to pull over. His headlights illuminated the area and satisfied himself that this would be a safe place to change a tire.

After turning left, Ennis brought the Mercedes to a full stop and thought to himself that was a wild ride and he was pleased with himself in that he had maneuvered the car to a safe area off the freeway. He turned off the engine. Since he was over six feet tall, he had to unfold himself from the little coupe so he could assess the situation. As he glanced at the front left tire, he could see it was entirely flat. Then he thought about the spare in the trunk and wondered if it was full of air. When opening the trunk lid, he could see that the spare was well inflated. He reflected on whether he should try to change the tire or should he call the auto club for service? Which would be quicker?

In order to be considerate of Stephanie, he gave her a call on his cell phone telling her that he had a flat tire and would be a little late. She asked where he was and he mentioned he was just below Mulholland Drive on Skirball Center off ramp of the 405. She said that wasn't far and she would come over to help. Ennis said he had the tire out and he should be at her place in 15 to 20 minutes. Stephanie was insistent to come over to provide him any assistance he might need. He tried to dissuade her but that was just wasting his time. He said, "OK whatever." He immediately returned to the task at hand which was the dirty job of changing a flat tire.

CHAPTER 2 SHOOTING OF ENNIS

Ennis was now 27 years old and felt he was self-reliant and able to handle himself. He remembered on several occasions he was with people who had flats and he helped change them. He reached in and spun the wing nut holding the spare in place. In less than a minute he had the spare out bouncing it on the ground. He rolled it forward to the front of the car and rested the spare against the front bumper.

At that moment he could see a small car pull up alongside and asked whether he needed any help. Ennis looked up at the Good Samaritans and said, "Everything is cool." He could see two guys in the front seat and a young woman in the back. Ennis thought to himself how generous it was for some strangers to offer to help. As they drove away, Ennis regrouped his thoughts and wondered if he shouldn't have accepted their help at least to shine light on the car so he could see what he was trying to do. At least he hoped that Stephanie would show up to provide him better lighting on the tire fixing project.

He knew the next part would be a little challenging in removing the jack from the trunk and placing it on the side of the car. When he inserted the jack in the round hole he remembered he had been warned by others to be extra careful so it didn't scratch the front fender while jacking the car up. He slowly jacked the car up to the point where the front left tire could spin freely.

Next, the lug wrench was retrieved and he started loosening the lug nuts on the rim. The wheel began to spin around and he couldn't break the lug nuts loose. He remembered one of his friends had mentioned that it was important to break the lug nuts loose before jacking the car all the way up. He leaned over to the jack and lowered it about an inch. Then he stood up and with all the strength he could muster he pushed down on the wrench. He knew that the lugs had been put on by using a power lug wrench so he leaned over and yanked downward with all of his might. The first lug moved slightly and another yank broke it loose. After that it was a piece of cake to loosen the others.

By then he saw some headlights reflecting off his car. He turned his head and could make out the shadowy figure of a Jaguar. He could barely recognize the lady inside but knew it had to be Stephanie. Putting the lug wrench down he wiped his hands together as though he was cleaning them but he could see his hands were greasy black. He walked over to the headlights and approached the driver's door. Stephanie was bundled up in her mink coat. She rolled the window down and looked at him and smiled, stating, "What a mess you got yourself into." Ennis couldn't help but laugh at his situation. His fingernails were full of grease and he didn't evoke the impression of a PhD. candidate. He exclaimed, "I like working on cars. It's fun."

Stephanie said, "How can I help?" Ennis looked toward his car and said, "I really could use some light on the car." He directed her to pull her Jaguar closer pointing the headlights to the area of the front left tire. By pulling into the street slightly, she was able to light up the front of the Mercedes. Now Ennis resumed fixing his flat tire. After removing the flat tire he rolled it back to the trunk and with a heave hoe, he threw it in the trunk. Proceeding to the front of the car he rolled the spare into place. All the lug bolts filled his hand as he started to screw each one onto the rim.

Since there wasn't much traffic in this area, the night air was hushed with a low roar from the 405 freeway slightly below. This silence was broken by a voice loudly stating, "Open the door or I will shot you." Ennis turned his head toward the speaker who was standing next to the driver's window of Stephanie's Jaguar. Since Ennis was looking into the bright headlights of Stephanie's car, he couldn't make out what was happening. He stood up from tightening the lug nuts. Before he could take a step toward the voice, Stephanie's car squealed passed him almost striking him. Reflectively, he jumped back and a blur of a Jaguar sped up the street toward Mulholland Drive.

Ennis turned his head toward this thin framed young man who was hard to see in all the darkness. The most Ennis could see was the silhouette of a figure approaching him. Ennis strained to see who this was. He appeared to have something in his right hand. Ennis's senses were in overload mode. Could it be a gun in his hand? The question was answered by the dark figure shouting out, "This is a robbery. Give me your money!" The voice seemed to be barking out orders with some type of European accent.

Ennis was caught by surprise. It didn't seem real. His eyes and ears were trying to pick up any clues. Why would someone want to rob a person with a flat tire?

Ennis hadn't been a victim of a robbery before and this entire flat tire affair hadn't put him in the best of moods. He didn't know what to say and do. Should he take his wallet out and give him all his money? But his hands were covered with dirt and grim and the last thing he wanted to do was put his dirty hands in his pockets and mess up his clothes.

He tried to ask what the robber really wanted. Was it the car? Was it his watch? Or was it just his wallet? The robber seemed frustrated by the delay and tried to impress his victim by sticking the gun closer to him. As both sides tried to figure what to do, the trigger was pulled and a bullet roared out of the revolver barrel and struck Ennis in the head knocking him off his feet. His body came to rest beside the driver's side of his car.

As Ennis fell to the pavement, his limp body was lite up by the headlights of Stephanie's car. As she slowly approached the robber, he seemed fixated like a deer facing headlights. Should he lean down and take Ennis' wallet? Or should he run since he couldn't make out whose car was approaching? With a slight hesitancy at first, he ran over to an awaiting car which sped off into the darkness.

As Stephanie returned she had seen a young white man wearing a light-colored watch cap who ran toward a car near the Park and Ride area. Her immediate attention was on Ennis who appeared to be lying motionless next to his car. She pulled up and jumped out and knelt next to Ennis. She could see the blood streaming down the pavement. She froze with fear not knowing if she was safe. She ran back to her car and grabbed her cellphone and dialed 9-1-1. Within minutes she was surrounded by police officers who were trying to obtain some type of description of the robber. Her mind was in a state of shock and a deep feeling of guilt. If only she hadn't sped off, Ennis might still be alive.

Just like in Charles Dickens ***Tale of Two Cities***, the beginning of the day had started out as the 'Best of Times,' but unfortunately, Ennis' death ended with the 'Worst of Times' for the Cosby family.

CHAPTER 3 WHO WAS ENNIS COSBY?

Ennis was many things to many people. He was well liked by everyone he came into contact with. His special greeting of "Hello Friend," spoke volumes of his warm welcoming disposition. What in his upbringing made him such a pleasant, sensitive individual? On April 15, 1969, he was born into a celebrity family with all the advantages that come along with that status. It was a large family with four sisters which forced Ennis to learn about dressing up and doing the things that girls enjoy.

The family was influenced by the fact that his father was busy with a career that demanded that he be away from the family. During Ennis's growing years, his dad had a hectic schedule working on his ***Fat Albert & the Cosby Kids*** TV show. By the time ***The Cosby Show*** took off in popularity, Ennis was 15 years old. Throughout the eight seasons it was one of the top TV shows when Ennis was teenager. One of the key characters in the show was the son named Theo Hustable, who mimicked Ennis' life.

Both Ennis and the TV character, Theo, were the same age with four sisters and he was experiencing academic problems in school. The character Theo had Dyslexia just like Ennis and was able to conquer the disability and go on to excel in college. Ennis didn't enjoy any privacy since the TV writers seem to copy his life in this Theo character.

Ennis did well in Grade School at George School in Newton, Pennsylvania which allowed him to go on to Morehouse College in Atlanta, Georgia. When he was diagnosed as having the learning disability of Dyslexia, he stated it was the best day of his life. Then it was understandable as to why he had problems reading and writing. At Morehouse, he received the help he needed and the sky was the limit as to what he could be.

Ennis could have rested on his family name as one of the most talked about families in America at that time. The strange thing was that he didn't have any desire to grab onto his father's coattails to climb his way into the entertainment industry. For some unexplained reason, Ennis was more comfortable in helping people who were not as fortunate as he was.

A demonstration of his desire to help others could be seen when he volunteered to teach Sunday school in the Bronx. He didn't have to do it but he found an interior satisfaction in serving others. In order to have a bigger impact, he realized he needed to have the education that would allow him to hold higher positions where he could help even more people. That was when he enrolled in the Graduate Studies at Columbia Teacher's College in New York.

His father was proud of Ennis's desire to help others. Bill Cosby couldn't have been more gratified that his son had followed the path of education to better himself.

His father regretted all the opportunities that he had as a young person which he didn't take advantage of.

CHAPTER 4

DISCARDING GUN

January 16, 1997, seemed like any other day in Los Angeles although slightly on the cool side. However, Russians who were students of history would know this was the date in 1547 when Ivan IV, better known as 'Ivan the Terrible,' was crowned czar of Russia. Mikhail Markhasev, who in 1989 with his mother had migrated here from Russia (technically the Ukraine) and had no memory of 'Ivan the Terrible.' His mind was fixated on what to do with the gun he had just used to kill someone in a botched robbery.

After the shooting, he ran over to the car driven by his friend, Eli Z, and jumped into the passenger seat. The getaway vehicle was an older VW Rabbit which could be described as slightly distinctive with flames painted on both front doors giving it a satanic look. When Mikhail got in the car he yelled at his buddy, "Get the hell out of here." Eli punched the accelerator as hard as he could making the car lurch forward but the engine wasn't tough enough to make the tires squeal.

The driver, Eli, sped over to the 'on ramp' of the 405 freeway going northbound. Eli kept looking in his rear-view mirror and didn't see any cars following them. Mikhail wanted to act like a big-time crook but didn't know exactly what to say. Eli's girlfriend was in the backseat and she looked scared as though she felt she was over her head as to what just happened. Mikhail, in some way, wanted to impress her as though they were the new Bonny and Clyde of Mulholland Drive. She didn't seem to be ready to play the role of 'Bonny Elizabeth Parker' who went out in a blaze of glory on May 23, 1934 in Bienville Parish, Louisiana.

As they proceeded down the hill into the San Fernando Valley, Mikhail directed Eli to proceed eastbound on the 101 Freeway. Mikhail was trying to figure out what he should be doing next in a botched robbery. He focused on the fact that he needed to get rid of the revolver. He didn't want to throw it in the trash. All he wanted was to find a place to hide the gun for several days until the incident blew over. Eli asked Mikhail, "Where do you want to go?" Mikhail didn't answer but was pondering the question. Eventually he responded that he knew of a park like area where he could hide the gun. He explained to Eli that he couldn't remember if it was Coldwater Canyon or Laurel Canyon but he knew it was one of the two.

Eli was looking at the freeway signs and he said, "Coldwater Canyon is coming up next." Mikhail looked out the passenger window and said it looked like the area. He said to Eli, "Turn off here at Coldwater." The car glided down the off ramp to a stop at the signal at Coldwater Canyon Avenue. They turned right and continued in the right-hand lane and slowly headed to Ventura Boulevard. Mikhail said, "There are a lot of trees and some type of river channel that runs through it." Mikhail was straining to look at the landscape and all of sudden he said, "Stop, pull into this driveway."

Eli stopped in front of a chain linked gate. At 1:30 a.m. there was stillness in the area and it was pitch black. To the left was a row of apartment buildings with only several bathroom frosted windows illuminated. No one was in the area and the silence was only broken by occasional cars driving by on Coldwater Canyon Avenue. Mikhail announced that this is a perfect place to hide the gun. He got out of the car and walked passed the gate and disappeared into the darkness. The park like setting was made up of dozens of tall eucalyptus trees which sheltered the view from the row of apartments. Without a flashlight Mikhail couldn't see exactly where he was but he climbed up a slight incline where the brush became thicker.

Mikhail leaned over on his knees and used his hands to feel through the brush. He felt a large amount of eucalyptus bark mixed with disintegrating leaves about a foot high. Pulling the gun out of his waistband with his right hand he took his left hand and removed the watch cap he had been wearing. He carefully wrapped the revolver in the watch cap so it was no longer visible. With his left hand he raised the debris up from the ground and slid the gun wrapped in the watch cap under the stack of decomposing leaves. With both hands he neatly sprinkled more leaves over the site where he had placed the gun. He took his hands and tried to tidy up the leaves so no one would notice that something was hidden below.

He turned around and walked back down the slight slope and headed back to the headlights of the car. When he returned to the car, he smiled at Eli, "Well that's done, let's get out of here." Mikhail was proud of himself in that he knew exactly what had to be done. He only wished he could share this moment with his fellow gang members.

While living in Orange County, he was a member of the 'Varrio Los Alamitos Street Gang.' Since he was the only non-Hispanic in the gang, he always felt that he had to prove himself. His fellow homeboys would be more than impressed with how smart he was in getting rid of the gun so it couldn't be traced back to him.

When he was back in the car he announced that they needed to go to their friend's place to find out what the news media was saying about the shooting. His buddy, Isaac, lived nearby so he told Eli to head over to Isaac's place. Eli very carefully backed out of the Flood Control driveway onto Coldwater Canyon without attracting any attention. They drove to Isaac's house and arrived unannounced around 2:00 a.m.

CHAPTER 5 CRIME SCENE INVESTIGATION

During those early morning hours the LAPD Robbery Homicide Division (RHD) was scrambling as to how to initiate the investigation. A team of detectives converged on the crime scene. Initially, they need to make an assessment as to the status of the victim. Should there be an attempt to revive the victim through heroics. In many shooting situations family members of the victim want everything and anything to be done to save their loved one. Here Ennis had been shot once through the head. The city paramedics had come out and made an assessment that Ennis was dead and couldn't be resuscitated.

The detectives have to make a critical decision of what to do about the body of the victim. Since Stephanie told the police exactly who the victim was, right from the get-go LAPD was on notice that they had a 'Celebrity Homicide.' The word continued to spread that Bill Cosby's son had been shot to death near the 405 Freeway. It wasn't long before the news media vans began converging from every angle. News crews were trying to get a close-up picture of Ennis' body lying on the pavement next to his car. Detectives tried to assemble a barricade to block the view of the body. As soon as the sun came up the news media helicopters were blanketed overhead trying to zoom in on the body. All the detectives could do was place a cover over the body.

Preserving the crime scene was first and foremost while reaching out to find any and all witnesses to the crime. The detectives had Stephanie C who had called the police and remained at the scene to provide information as to what happened. Her statements made it sound like a robbery. She related that the suspect tapped on her window and said, "Get out or I'll shoot you." The detectives listened to her statement but it didn't completely add up. Ennis still had on his wrist an expensive Rolex watch and two $20 bills in his pocket.

It didn't go unnoticed that Stephanie was wearing a short mink coat with high heel shoes. What was her relationship to Ennis Cosby who was 27 and she was 47? She indicated that they had just recently met at the Chateau Marmont Hotel in Hollywood while both were at two separate functions occurring at the famed hotel. She said that Ennis had recently broken up with a longtime girlfriend and he wanted to talk to her about it.

Seasoned RHD detectives have heard every story in the book. The explanation that Ennis was going to her place at 1:00 a.m. to just talk had to be met with some skepticism. The detectives didn't want to presuppose the relationship, but they wanted to get past the point of considering her as a possible suspect. Could there have been some type of domestic violence between them? Could she have picked this isolated location to shoot Ennis?

The more they talked to Stephanie they realized that in no way was she a suspect but she was a genuine witness who had been present at this tragic event. At that moment, the detectives needed to pick her memory as to everything that happened. Next, they needed to put out an all-points bulletin as to the shooter and the car he got away in. The entire shooting had a traumatic impact on her. She wanted to be helpful but she seemed to be detached from what was going on around her. When they pressed her for a description of the suspect, she would phrase her answer by saying that it was dark and it all happened so quickly.

One of the detectives took her to the side and tried to calm her down with some small talk. Then he meticulously asked specific questions as to the suspect. Her comments were general in nature that the suspect was a male, white, with a thin face and with a sharp nose. As to his hair, she indicated that he had a watch cap on which was light in color. Later, the detectives would have her sit down with a forensic artist to develop a composite sketch which would be used by law enforcement.

The description of the suspect wasn't as helpful as the detectives would like but they had to take what they could get. More questions were asked as to what she was doing earlier in the evening. She related that she had been over at her sister's place after which she returned home. That was when she received a call from Ennis. He had called her on several other occasions late in the evening. This time he didn't just want to talk over the phone but wanted to personally see her. She told him to come on over to her Sherman Oaks house. A short time later she received another call from him explaining he had a flat tire near Mulholland Drive, just off of the 405 Freeway. Since this was just a short distance from her place, she offered to come by to help him out.

Since it was cold out and sporadically raining, she reached into her hall closet and grabbed the warmest wrap she could find, which was her short mink coat.

Hurriedly, she didn't change her high heel shoes and went out to her Jaguar parked in the driveway. She didn't have to give much thought where to go since it was less than a mile from her place. When she turned off Skirball Center Drive she could see Ennis changing the flat tire.

She pulled up from behind his Mercedes and he immediately walked over to her driver's window. After a few words he asked her to pull up closer and shine the jag's headlights on the area where he was working. After several minutes she heard a tap tap on her driver's window and looked up to see this thin young man with a gun in his hand. That was when he said, "Open the door or I'll shoot you." She tried to explain her reaction which was to hit the button to lock the doors. Since she had the engine running in order to have the warmth from the heater, all she had to do was put the car in drive and stomp on the accelerator.

She tried to justify her reaction for considering flight in place of complying with the suspect's command. The next thing she realized was the feeling of the Jaguar accelerating forward. She listened for any popping sound from the gun which she could not hear except for the engine racing as the car rocketed toward Mulholland Drive. She looked back through the rear-view mirror but couldn't make out what was happening since it was dark and no street lights were on. As she reached Mulholland Drive, she made a wide U turn so she was facing down Skirball Drive. Looking through the darkness she could make out the outline of Ennis' car. Two figures were standing next to the car but she was too far away to see or hear what was going on.

Should she call 9-1-1 or was it some type of joke? She felt all alone without anyone to lean on. Her reaction was to slowly return to where Ennis was. As she gradually drove down she could make out that the other man was running from

Ennis's car. It looked like he was heading to a Park and Ride parking lot on the other side of the road. Although her headlights illuminated Ennis' car, she couldn't get a good look at the man running away.

As she drove closer she could see Ennis lying on the pavement not appearing to be moving. When she was paralleled with the Mercedes, she stopped to make an assessment of the situation. That was when she jumped out of car and went to the aid of Ennis. She abruptly stopped talking to the detective. Tears started welling up in her frightened eyes. After a short pause she continued by relating to the detective that all she could think about was calling 9-1-1. The detective thanked her for her cooperation and said that they would be in touch with her to arrange a meeting with her and the forensics composite artist. She asked if the police could withhold her identity since she was frightened by the shooting. The detectives' response was that they would try to keep her name from the news media.

The forensic team was scurrying around searching for any clues they could find. No one was able to find a shell casing which indicated that it might have been a revolver which was used in the shooting. One of the detectives asked that the spare tire be removed from the trunk and taken to the lab to test it to see what caused the flat. Was it a real a flat tire or had it been an act of vandalism?

The photographer was given some instructions from the detectives as to some special shots they wanted. They included photos of Ennis' hands showing that they were greasy and dirty indicating someone who was working on a car. Since Stephanie C indicated that the suspect ran to the Park and Ride parking area they had detectives check on the cars that were still parked there. Further, they asked that the two pay phones be checked out and their phone numbers written down.

Since the detectives didn't have a suspect or a good description of a suspect or even a good description on the get-away car, the detectives wanted to be as thorough in their searching of the crime scene. The media was putting pressure on the police department to hold a news conference. The police chief at that time was Willy Williams who wanted to hold a news conference by the afternoon in order to get the public involved in helping track down the killer. By the time of the news conference the main source of information was basically what they had learned from Stephanie C.

At the time of Chief Williams briefing, the media had shown the photo of the mysterious woman in the short mink coat prancing around in her high heels. Naturally the media wanted to know her name so she could be interviewed. The Chief didn't reveal her name but the media started their own investigation to find out her name.

With the news media using the killing of Ennis Cosby as the main story, the entire country was made aware of the shooting. As a result, there were many leads that came into the RHD detectives. One clue involved a Tracy W, who was at a friend's house, (Gabe D) when three people left. One of them was wearing a dark colored watch cap. The three of them left at 12:20 a.m. and were only two miles from the site of the shooting. (Tracy believed that the people were going out to 'jack' someone in order to get money to purchase drugs.) The detectives got the name of the three people; Mikhail Markhasev, Eli Z, and Eli's girlfriend, Sara Ann P.

This witness couldn't put them at the crime scene and the watch cap was a different color than the one Stephanie had described. There wasn't enough to connect these people to the shooting. This was one of many clues that led to nothing useful.

CHAPTER 6 KILLER HAS A PROBLEM

Two days after the shooting, Mikhail felt like the walls were closing in on him. Did he do the right thing by disposing of the gun? What if someone found it? Had he sufficiently wiped the gun so his fingerprints were definitely not on it? The only way he could put his mind at ease was to go back and retrieve the gun before some kid would find it while playing in the park. The year was 1997, and the Spice Girls were the big rage with their songs like ***Wannabe*** and ***Say You'll Be There***. That may have been an omen for Mikhail in that he definitely 'Wannabe be a Gangster' as well as hoping the gun would still be there where he placed it.

But Mikhail suffered from the lack of having wheels. In other words, he didn't have a car nor did he have access to a car. He learned the hard way that he had to be nice to people since he was always begging someone to give him a ride. Since Orange County was where he called home, he needed to talk someone into giving him a ride to and from the San Fernando Valley some 35 miles away. As he reflected on the long trip he wondered how he would explain the need for the trip. By this time, he realized that he needed someone he could confide in. His homies could be trusted but no one had a car for such a long trip.

Mikhail remembered an old buddy by the name of Michael Chang who had a shady background but he could be totally trusted. So Mikhail called Michael and it wasn't long before he was agreeable to help Mikhail but there was one big problem. Michael didn't have a car and no one would loan him a car. Mikhail felt that the Spice Girls "***Say You'll Be There***" was not the song he was hearing. Apparently, Michael Chang recognized the desperation in Mikhail's voice. Michael volunteered that he knew someone who had a car but he would have to pay him for the gas.

Chang said he would call Chris So to see if he would be willing to make the trip for a price. Mikhail nodded in agreement that he had money he could pay the driver. With a little phone tag, Michael was able to track down Chris So. Chris wasn't keen about going to the San Fernando Valley but he needed his car gassed up so if someone was willing to fill up the car's tank then they could be on their way.

With a full gas tank, the motley crew of Mikhail and Michael Chang were being chauffeured by a tall, lanky Chris So who had no idea why he was headed to the San Fernando Valley. Since Chris was literally in the driver's seat, he started asking questions like where do you want to go? Why do you want to go there? Mikhail was reluctant to say too much since he truly didn't know Chris So from any stranger. Mikhail was sufficiently desperate to get a ride to find the gun that he didn't want to alienate the driver, Chris So.

What could he say to gain the cooperation of the driver but not to say too much? Using some gang talk he said, "I shot a n----(black man) it's all over the news." Then he went on to relate what his problem was. "I got to hide- this is really big." This frightened the driver as to what he was getting himself into. Mikhail followed up by saying he needed them to help him find the gun he used. He never used the words that he had shot Ennis Cosby but Chris So didn't need the picture framed, he clearly got the picture.

The conversation in the car focused on the question, where are we going? Mikhail couldn't give a specific address but said that he needed to go to somewhere off of Coldwater Canyon, South of the 101 Freeway. Chris So responded that he knew that general area and he made his way through the freeways of Los Angeles, coming out on the old Ventura Freeway designated the 101. As they approached the Coldwater Canyon freeway sign, Mikhail said, "That's it." Immediately Chris turned off the 101 heading south on Coldwater Canyon Avenue.

Mikhail rolled down the window in the backseat and was staring out at the rows of apartment houses that all looked alike. He made the comment that everything looks different in the daylight. He kept instructing Chris So to slow down so he could visualize in his mind what he had seen on the night in question and what he was observing now. They went over a small bridge with a flood control channel below it. He shook his head and Chris continued driving. By now they were approaching the large thoroughfare of Ventura Boulevard which Mikhail knew was too far to the South. Out of fear that he wasn't going to be able to find the location, he snapped at the driver and accused him of going too far.

The driver, Chris, caught himself from saying, "Hey dude I'm doing a favor for you. Don't yell at me." Mikhail realized that he was being too snappy and changed his tone by saying, "Let's go back." The traffic at this intersection of Coldwater and Ventura was a nightmare to go through since the Sportsman's Lodge is on one corner and a large Ralph's Market is on the other side. At that point, there was a steady stream of traffic coming down from the Mulholland Drive area just up the hill. Chris was able to find a place to make a U-turn; now heading northbound on Coldwater Canyon.

After passing Ventura Boulevard, Mikhail was intently looking from right to left to see if there was something he recognized. Then he saw the chain linked gate which looked familiar and shouted to Chris to pull into the little driveway in front of the gate. As the car came to a stop Mikhail surveyed the park like area next to the flood control channel. He remarked in the daylight it all looked so much larger. He directed everyone to get out of the car and told them to follow him as he walked down a slight slope to a grassy area.

Mikhail stood in the middle of the park and drew a complete blank as to where he had hidden the gun with the watch cap. He remembered the leaves and bark he used to cover the gun. Then he directed the others to help him search. They had this puzzled look like 'Do I look like someone who wants to become accessory to murder?' In order to give the appearance of cooperation, Chris So headed to a clump of trees and pretended to kick his feet through the piles and piles of leaves. Michael Chang proceeded to the flood control channel and walked along its curvy fence reaching down to pick up cans and bottles.

After ten minutes of searching, everyone re-congregated near the chain link gate. The logical question raised was what are we exactly looking for? In order to get the others to assist, Mikhail explained that he wrapped the revolver in a watch cap and placed it deeply in the leaves and debris under a bunch of trees. The three of them divided up and tried to do a more thorough search. After a half hour passed, Mikhail became depressed as to the fruitless effort to find the gun. Could it be that someone had already found the gun? Had it been turned over to the police? Or could this just be the wrong place?

They continued searching and finally Mikhail realized that after an hour he had to face the fact that the gun wasn't going to be found. There was some satisfaction that if they couldn't find it maybe he had done a good job of hiding it on the night of the shooting. They all returned to the car and all were disappointed that the objective of their mission had been a failure. It was time to return to Orange County where they called home. All the way home Mikhail complained that they would have to return another day and try again to find the gun. Throughout the drive back Chris So seemed to detect that Mikhail had become obsessed with relocating the gun. It was as though Mikhail had a premonition that the gun was going to be his downfall.

CHAPTER 7 NATIONAL ENQUIRER STEPS IN

Weeks went by turning into months as the winter became spring without any arrests in the killing of Ennis Cosby. The pressure was on LAPD to quickly solve the case. Media elements hinted that if the victim had been white there would be a more concerted effort to catch the killer. Maybe more detectives were needed to be assigned the case? Mistrust by certain groups painted the LAPD as being incompetent in their investigation.

During this entire time, the Cosby family was consumed by an allegation that Bill Cosby had fathered a 'Love Child.' There were lawsuits going back and forth which complicated the media picture of who could possibly be involved. Mr. Cosby's wholesome reputation was beginning to unravel.

Since no money was taken from Ennis, there were those who dismissed the theory that it was a 'robbery gone bad.' Could it be someone out to get Bill Cosby since he had his share of detractors? The city fathers of Los Angeles were staunch supporters of Bill Cosby and didn't want the reputation of such a famous icon to be blemished by any type of scandal.

The detectives of Robbery Homicide Division had to feel they were in a glass bowl with everyone taking pot shots at them. At times homicide detectives have to have thick skin when all the leads turn to quicksand as they sink deeper in the hole of doubt. The media started doing the 'psychic' routine by interviewing supernatural spiritualists who have some type of mythical vision as to who the killer might be. The media will ask the detectives if they have checked out the information the psychic has provided. The detectives recognize this slippery slope. If they say "No", then they are accused of not following through on all the clues. If they say "Yes, we have worked with the psychic", the general population shake their heads in disbelief and think no wonder the cops haven't caught the killer.

The RHD detectives were greeted by the news that the National Enquirer had posted a $100,000 reward for anyone who came forth with information that lead to the arrest and conviction of the killer of Ennis Cosby. How should the police department react when confronted with the help of a tabloid who many refer to as a scandal rag with no credibility? This was insulting to some to have LAPD pitted against the National Enquirer to see who could solve the case first. However, there were some sitting on the sideline who believed in the old adage that 'Money Talks.'

The detectives continued with the investigation they had in progress and resented that a low level tabloid was using this ploy to gain publicity. They ignored this side show and hoped that old 'gumshoe detective work' eventually would pay off. Within a few days, the National Enquirer called LAPD and said that they had a phone number of someone who seemed to know something. Since the detectives had run out of productive leads, one of them wrote down the phone number and called it expecting to hear some bizarre story worthy of $100,000.

The man on the other end of the line was Chris So who lived in Orange County. He wanted to play a cat and mouse game of not revealing too much so Mikhail wouldn't be able to figure out he was the so-called informant. Chris was struggling with his conscience as to saying only enough to get the reward but not too much to have Mikhail's gang coming after him. The detective was getting a far-fetched story that someone had asked him to look for a gun that was used in a big murder.

The person on the line was captivating the detective's interest. Now the detective was playing the role of disbelief and asking this Mr. So what this person told him. The caller said he told me, "I shot a n------, it's all over the news. I got to hide- this is really big". By now the detective knew he was on to something, but the person was not giving up the name of the shooter quite yet. The detective took a different tack of asking about the so called location where he had helped look for the gun. The detective put the person on the defensive by saying "Okay, why don't you show us where you looked?" The caller said they never found the gun and the shooter said he was going to go back to look for the gun.

The detective had the caller where he wanted him. Now the caller was going to have to meet with the detectives and show them where he helped to search for the gun. If this was BS, they would soon know. Things were set up for this Mr. So to take the detectives to the little park alongside the flood control channel.

Apparently, Mr. So was starting to image the $100,000 check in his pocket. They all met off of Coldwater Canyon near Ventura Boulevard. Mr. So wanted to be cooperative only to the extent to get the money but not enough to be in the cross hairs of Mikhail's gun. He walked over to the park area and pointed out all the places that they had looked for the gun. The detectives could see the mammoth amount of territory that needed to be searched.

A group of detectives spread out and started canvassing the area not certain what they were looking for. Mr. So had indicated that the object was a gun and that it was buried in the ground or hidden in the trunk of a rotted out tree. The detectives tried to envision whether the gun was wrapped in something like a towel. After an hour, several of the seasoned detectives regrouped and expressed some skepticism as to whether this was more of a 'search for a needle in a haystack.' Mr. So wasn't being overly candid. Maybe he came up with this story only to receive the reward. And who was saying that the gun hadn't already been found by the shooter or some young person playing in the park.

The lead detective could see this search exercise hadn't convinced any converts to the idea that they were hot on the trail of the gun that killed Ennis Cosby. Someone made a halfhearted comment that they needed a bunch of soldiers to march shoulder to shoulder across the park area. That raised a smile from the older detectives who had done their fair share of futile searches. All of a sudden there was a revelation moment when the head detective asked the group for the phone number of the LAPD training academy.

CHAPTER 8

SEARCHING FOR GUN

The phone call was made to the academy asking the availability of the cadets to help out in the Cosby case investigation. The Academy sergeant thought for a moment, this could be a learning experience that these new recruits would forever remember. The sergeant responded with how many do you need, where, and when? When the old-time detectives heard they were being replaced by cadets, there was a mixed reaction. But since it seemed such a futile exercise, the detectives' swallowed their pride and were happy to give the cadets the chance to prove their skills of being the new *Colombo* (Peter Falk) solving cases in the most mysterious ways.

Within an hour a series of LAPD vans came roaring up to the chain link gate. Out jumped the cadets who looked like locust ready to swarm over the park. The lead detective knew he had one chance to get this search right so he told the cadets' sergeant he needed the cadets to line up shoulder to shoulder in front of the chain link gate stretching to both sides of the park. Within seconds the training sergeant was barking out orders for the cadets to line up in a row to which the cadets scrambled to take their positions next to each other. Instantaneously, the cadets were in a perfect line that would have put the 'honor guard' to shame at the Arlington Cemetery.

The lead detective stood out in front of the cadets and told them that he wanted them to march arm and arm looking down at their feet searching for a gun. The sergeant gave the order to march slowly and the line moved across the park like they were practicing 'Line Dancing' in slow motion. The plan worked well and the old-time detectives were pleased not having to do this tedious job. Since they say the 'proof is in the pudding' it seemed that all this precision marching hadn't turned up any gun.

The cadets' march hadn't been able to go through the wooded area on the high banks of the park. It was decided to have the cadets come back in a cluster swarming around the various trees. As the cadets waded through the brush and thick trees there was a faint voice from a cadet saying, "I think I found something." The cadets hearing this started to surround their colleague. It seemed like a group of football players jumping on top of each other to celebrate the winning touchdown.

The lead detective panicked in that he didn't want anything touched and wanted the area treated like a crime scene. The sergeant had to think that the lectures he had given to the cadets about preserving a crime scene apparently hadn't made much of an impression on them. With considerable yelling by the sergeant, the cadets moved away so the homicide detectives could find the cadet who had discovered the 'Something.'

When the detective leaned down he could see that the gun was wrapped in a watch cap. Now with latex gloves the detective examined the gun and could see that it was a revolver in which one bullet had been fired. The detective could see that the bullets fit the size of the one removed from Ennis' body. The detective asked the cadet who had found it to replace it exactly where he found it. One of the CIS photographer's was called over to photograph the location where the gun was actually found.

The lead detective shook his head in puzzlement how lucky they were to find the gun. However, if it hadn't been for the eagerness of the academy cadets, the gun would never have been found. Everything had fallen into place. It was clear that Mr. Chris So was credible and obviously had more information that the detectives needed to extract from him. Now it was time to have a serious conversation with Mr. So. They needed the name of the person who had asked him to help look for the gun. The cadet's discovery was crucial and to think that it all came about because of a lead from the National Enquirer. All of a sudden those demeaning comments about that 'tabloid rag' had to be replaced with words of enthusiastic admiration for their team effort in helping to solve the case.

CHAPTER 9

INVESTIGATION OF MIKHAIL MARKHASEV

Mikhail Markhasev should be the 'Poster Child' for America's softer and gentler immigration policy. He was born out of wedlock in Lvov in the Ukraine. His mother had some basic skills as a pattern maker. Raising a son was a struggle for her so she married Valyri Markhasev. He was willing to adopt Mikhail and give him his surname. Life was as good as it could be in the Ukraine but unfortunately, his parents divorced. Three years later, when Mikhail was 11, his mother decided to move to the USA settling in the West Hollywood area. This region was a popular Russian enclave in Los Angeles.

Mikhail excelled in school and was thought of as a gifted student at John Burroughs Junior High School. He was a popular kid who never caused any disciplinary problems. However, there are pivotal points in everyone's life. For Mikhail it occurred in 1995, when his family moved to Orange County. This should have been an enormous plus for him since Orange County is a conservative area where the old world values are appreciated.

It's unknown exactly what the changing moment in his life was. Because of his small stature and his sharp facial features, he was given the nickname of 'Pee-wee' since he resembled the comedian Pee-wee Herman who had a short physique with pointed features. At the beginning, it was taken as a compliment since Pee-wee Herman was a very popular comic fictional character starring in many TV programs and movies. They were titled Pee-wee's Big Adventure; Pee-wee's Playhouse; and Sesame Street. His character was thought of as a flamboyant funny guy. Unfortunately for Mr. Herman, his stardom crashed and burned when he was arrested for indecent exposure in a dark and dingy theater, jacking off in front of others. The Mr. Clean image rapidly went down the drain. From that point on, being called Pee-wee Herman was a derogatory term for a "dirty old man."

No one knows for sure how Mikhail took the change in character for his moniker 'Pee-wee.' But at this same time, Mikhail became more involved in one of the local gangs. Did he do it for protection or was it a way he could prove how rough and tough he could be? No one knows for sure. His gang affiliation was with the 'Los Alamitos Street Gang.' What was peculiar was that the gang members were Hispanics and a small Ukrainian kid didn't seem to fit in.

But Mikhail tried to adapt and started spouting off the hatred for "Blacks' his Hispanics gang disliked. He started interspersing racial epithets in his vocabulary to prove that he belonged to the gang mentality. In order to convince his homies that he was the 'Real Deal', he took part in an attack on two black men at a gas station in Los Alamitos. One of the men was stabbed in the arm and Mikhail and several of his gang members were arrested for the attack. Since Mikhail was only 16 at the time, he was sentenced to six months at a juvenile correctional facility.

By this time the demure studious honor's student had decided to change the direction of his life. He chose to follow the gang life; involving himself in drugs and alcohol and his personality became more belligerent and predatory.

In order to become the best of what he wanted to be, he familiarized himself with guns and spent time practicing his marksmanship at the Target Practice Range. He worked out at the gym trying to bulk up through weight lifting. A new Mikhail Markhasev had been created and was a ticking time bomb about to go off at any time.

Originally in their investigation, the detectives had received word that a person by the name of Mikhail Markhasev might be involved. This never went anywhere since no one could place him at the crime scene. Later, when the police received the information from Chris So regarding Mikhail's possible involvement in the Cosby shooting, the detectives were more than eager to check him out. When they arrested him he didn't provide any useable statements that the detectives could use against him in court.

But the police had one Ace up their sleeve. When they looked at the composite sketch it looked so similar to Mikhail. Since Stephanie C had been the one who helped to create it, the detectives were anxious to arrange a line-up in which she could attend. The detectives worked with the Men's Central Jail in setting up a time for a live line-up. All the logistics were worked out and Stephanie C was brought in and took a seat in the audience. On the back wall of the stage were the numbers 1-6.

A thick glass wall separated the participants in the line-up from the audience. The one-way glass prevented the suspect in the line-up from seeing who was attending the line-up. The suspect's attorney is permitted to be present but cannot interfere with the line-up. A prosecutor from the DA's Office is present to make sure the proper procedure is followed. Since the detectives have been doing line-ups, they know the proper procedure to follow and seldom does a prosecutor have to be involved except as an observer.

Stephanie C was read the legal precautionary language required in all line-ups. Then six men all dressed exactly alike in jailhouse attire wearing dark watch caps marched out from the left side, filling the entire stage. All the detectives and attorneys were out of Stephanie's view. For all who were waiting on the sideline, the tension in the room couldn't be higher. If she identifies Mikhail, the detectives would be elated since this would mean that the case will be given to the DA on a 'Silver Platter'. The DA was anxious since a positive ID by Stephanie C would assure the case would be a slam dunk. It doesn't get any better if a person from the crime scene can identify the killer.

After 20 minutes the line-up was over and Stephanie was asked to fill out the identification form. All eyes were on Stephanie writing on the form. No one was close enough to see what she had written down. The detective conducting the line-up had Stephanie sign the form and it was taken to a photocopy machine and multi-copies were made.

Unceremoniously, the detective came back and handed out the copies. The head LAPD detective was given his copy and he quietly perused it as his face went from and excited red to ashen gray. The prosecutor got her copy and her nervous smile turned to a frown of "Oh my God". The only one who seemed jubilant was

Markhasev's attorney who looked like he had just won the mega million dollar lottery.

It wasn't just the fact that Stephanie didn't identify Markhasev, but that she made a tentative ID of someone who was totally unrelated to the case. This was like a double whammy. However, with the fact that Stephanie tried to identify someone else was like taking a steak knife and stabbing it in the heart of the prosecution's case. The day of this live line-up was definitely not a good day for the DA.

Earlier, when Mikhail was arrested, a search warrant was issued for his residence. One of the items listed for seizure was any watch caps. When Mikhail's room was searched, several watch caps were found. This didn't prove much except it laid a foundation for the fact that Mikhail liked to wear watch caps.

To follow up on watch caps the one that was found in the park with the gun wrapped in it was examined and placed in an evidence envelope. No thought was given for a forensic examination of the watch cap. It wasn't until a year later that the watch cap was examined and a strand of human hair was found stuck inside. The hair was examined by the Crime Lab for possible DNA. They were able to come up with a match to Mikhail Markhasev. This was an unexpected find and a big plus for the prosecution.

Since Ennis was shot once meant there would be only one ballistic piece of evidence (the slug recovered by the coroner from Ennis head) that could be compared to the exemplar which was fired from the recovered gun. Fortunately, the Crime Lab didn't have any difficulty matching up the gun to the victim.

As time went by, the gang detectives received word from an informant that Mikhail was sending letters to his homies describing his involvement in the Cosby case. The detectives then were on the lookout for letters that Mikhail had written.

They were tipped off that some letters could be found in the house trash of jailhouse informant's girlfriend. Others were obtained from a jailer who had received envelops from Mikhail to be mailed. This correspondence was forwarded to the detectives instead of mailing them.

These letters included incriminating statements such as, "It was a Robbery gone bad". "Went to rob a connection (Drug Dealer) and obviously found something else". The letter was signed by the moniker "Pee-wee". The next step was for the detectives to find a handwriting expert who could say that the writing was consistent with and matched Mikhail's handwriting.

Undoubted Markhasev's attorney warned him from talking to any of his fellow jail mates since they could be informants. He should have been made aware that writing letters could be seized by the jailers. The question was why would Mikhail write such letters to his homies? Apparently in Mikhail's gang world, a gangster wants to be respected. One the best ways to gain respect is by bragging to his fellow gang members of all of his accomplishments. The prosecution was pleased that the detectives had seized these letters and they would be part of the corner stone to support their case.

CHAPTER 10

MIKHAIL'S FRIENDS

After the arrest of Mikhail, the detectives remembered the original information they had received that Mikhail had left Gabe's place with **Eli Z** and **Sara P**. When the two were interviewed they sang like birds. They made it clear that they didn't know what Mikhail was up to. They wanted everyone to know that they didn't have anything to do with the robbery/ murder.

Later at the grand jury proceeding, Sara P (22) testified that she and her boyfriend met up with Mikhail at Gabe's place and decided to leave looking for a narcotics dealer. Then they ended up off of the 405 Freeway approaching a 'Park and Ride' parking lot. There they saw a man standing next to his car with a flat tire. She remembered Eli yelling out to the man if he needed any help to which the man replied, "Everything is Cool". After that exchange, they pulled in and parked in the 'Park and Ride.' Mikhail exited the car and casually walked over to two pay phones to try to call a dope dealer. When he wasn't successful, he tried to call Gabe for more information but he couldn't reach Gabe after calling twice.

Next thing she knew was hearing what sounded like a car backfiring. She didn't think much of it until Mikhail came running back to their car and he said nervously, "Let's go. We've got to get out of here. Let's go." She remembered that her boyfriend, Eli Z, yelled at him, "What's going on?" And Mikhail didn't answer as they continued to drive away by entering the freeway.

Sara continued to testify to the Grand Jury that they continued to drive on the freeways until Mikhail told Eli to turn off and they traveled to a wooded area like a park in North Hollywood. There, Mikhail left the car by himself and seemed to hide something in the brushy undergrowth area. After that, they drove over to Isaac's girlfriend's place and Mikhail turned on the TV. Mikhail remained fixated on the TV into the morning and he seemed obsessed with learning all the information about the shooting. As it became light outside there was new sensational information announced that the victim who was shot was identified as Bill Cosby's son, Ennis.

By this time, Eli Z became angry because he realized what Mikhail had done. All Mikhail kept saying to himself was, "Why did it have to happen? Why did I have to do it?" After the shooting Eli and Sara tried to distance themselves from Mikhail.

At the same time the detectives were obtaining useful statements from the two occupants of the car, the detectives had scored the big prize by finding the gun. With that came the interviews with Chris So and Michael Chang. Michael Chang knew Mikhail since they had been in a juvenile detention facility together. Mikhail felt comfortable revealing to Michael Chang what really happened. He knew that Michael Chang could be trusted since he was a fellow inmate that he had spent considerable time with while serving his sentence at the juvenile camp.

Chang testified at the Grand Jury hearing that Mikhail had confided in him as to what had happened. He testified Mikhail explained that he had walked over to

Cosby, stuck a gun in his face and demanded money. Cosby told Mikhail that no one had ever pointed a gun at him before, and he said to "kick back, to hold on". Mikhail related that Cosby didn't get his wallet out fast enough. Chang testified that, "It was kind of like, 'Can you believe what he said to me'?" Then Mikhail said, "I just blasted him."

When Chang arranged for Chris So to drive him and Mikhail to the North Hollywood area, there was a conversation in the car. That was when Mikhail said, "I killed a N----: It's big. It's all over the news." That was when Chang uttered, "You killed Cosby!" At that moment Mikhail shut up and didn't want to do any more talking about the shooting.

The detectives were fat, dumb and happy. How could it get any better? Well, little did the detectives know what would soon wipe the smiles off their faces?

CHAPTER 11 PHONE CALLS

Phone calls would be an important element of the prosecution's evidence in the case. These days much can be learned from cell phone activity such as where a cell phone was used to make a call or receive a call. Back in 1997, many people relied on the use of pagers. The purpose was to notify a person with the pager to get in contact with the caller. The prosecutors in the Cosby case relied heavily on Markhasev's use of his pager and cell phone activity of the various parties. In essence, the corroboration the prosecution needed was basically supplied by these electronic devices.

First off, the detectives had received word from Eli Z and Sara that they had gone to the Skirball Center 'Park and Ride' off the 405 Freeway. The purpose for stopping there was to use the pay phone next to the entrance of the 'Park and Ride'. Mikhail, with Eli Z and Sara, were trying to locate a narcotic dealer they could rip off but were having trouble finding his location.

Mikhail used the pay phone to call Gabe D's house to ask for more information. The detectives obtained the phone records for both pay phones at the 'Park and Ride'. By examining the phone records they could see that a call from one of the pay phones was made to a Ticor Title Company at 1:15 a.m. and another call one minute later at 1:16 a.m., moments before the shooting. The detectives were suspicious. Why would anyone call a Title Company after midnight when they would not be open?

One of the detectives looked at the phone number of the Title Company which seemed familiar. He tried to remember where he had seen it before. He glanced at a series of phone numbers and noticed that Gabe D's house phone appeared to have the same phone number. He compared the two numbers and discovered that Gabe's phone number was merely one digit different from that of the Title Company.

That was when the detectives realized that Mikhail had made those two calls to the Title Company by mistake when he was trying to reach Gabe. One of the elements the prosecution needed to prove was that the suspect had the opportunity to commit the crime. What that proved was that Mikhail was standing within 400 feet of where Ennis was shot at the exact time Stephanie C said that the shooting occurred around 1:20 a.m. In other words, Mikhail did have the Opportunity to commit the crime since he was there. Unfortunately for the prosecution, the Title Company's number was one digit off. It would have been better if the number called was that of Gabe's, but a prosecutor was willing to use it as incriminating evidence even though it wasn't a perfect match.

The phone and pager records showed that Mikhail's mother was continually paging him from 7:00 a.m. to 9:50 a.m. the morning after the shooting. Then he called her back and spoke with her for a short time. Obviously, the police didn't know what he and his mother were talking about but all afternoon she was paging him and he would call her back within five minutes. There was something concerning him in which he wanted to talk to his mother.

However, the one area in which the phone calls were helpful was when Michael Chang and Chris So were talking to the police about when they were contacted by Mikhail to go look for the gun. The phone records showed that Mikhail, on the afternoon after the shooting, called Chang at 4:55 p.m. and later called him back at 5:04 p.m. and spoke to him for 31 minutes. This corresponded to what Chang told the police in which he said that Mikhail asked for transportation to North Hollywood but he couldn't help him out since he didn't have a car.

Chang related to the detectives that he tried to think of what friends and associates he knew who had a car to take them to North Hollywood. Chang recalled his old friend Chris So who did have a car so he gave him a phone call shortly after talking to Mikhail. This was all verified by the phone records which showed that at 5:35 p.m. Chang called Chris So and talked for two minutes. Again the next day, Chris So called Chang back at 5:27 p.m. and on the following day at 11:19 a.m., all of which the detectives could verify by the phone records. Then on January 18, 1997, the phone records showed Chang calling Mikhail to get together to look for the gun.

The phone records weren't only helpful to show Mikhail's activities but were very vital to set the timeline of the events leading up to the shooting. From the phone records of Ennis Cosby and Stephanie C it could be established the exact time when he called her to tell her he would be late since he had a flat tire. That occurred at 1:00 a.m. and we know that she called 9-1-1 for help at 1:24 a.m. By having those two times it could be inferred that the shooting happened around 1:20 a.m..

The phone and pager records were just one more tool the detectives used to establish a realistic timeline when all these events occurred. The prosecutor knew that many of the witnesses weren't going to remember the exact time of various events but the phone records provided them with a reference point to relate the sequence of events.

CHAPTER 12

PREPARING FOR TRIAL

The news media had picked up the Cosby story and were anxious to report on it. They could see a new sequel to the O.J. Simpson debacle. They were hoping to make it into a new soap opera that would fill daytime television for the next year. The DA's Office had been burned severely by the O.J. Simpson case with its gavel to gavel TV coverage. Judge David Perez (who had been assigned the Markhasev case) could easily remember what happened to poor Judge Lance Ito with the famous 'Dancing Ito's' from late night TV fame.

So when the news media pressed for another gavel to gavel coverage, there was no stomach for it. The District Attorney, Gil Garcetti, knew his days were numbered after the O.J. Simpson case and he wasn't about to go through another media circus on the Cosby case. Anne Ingalls, the trial prosecutor, knew of the dangers of having cameras in the courtroom. The Defense attorney was from the Alternate Public Defenders Office and he certainly didn't need or want the publicity that came along with the televising of the proceedings.

When Judge Perez ruled on no TV cameras in the courtroom, the media wasn't happy but this was a God send for the prosecution in that the witnesses wouldn't be as reluctant to testify. In this case, the prosecution was going to call a number of witnesses who could be influenced by the threats from Mikhail Markhasev's street gang.

After the Grand Jury hearing, the DA's Office had to make a determination whether to seek the Death Penalty. Before trial, the DA's Office announced that after reviewing and weighing the Aggravating and Mitigating factors, they believed that based on the defendant's young age of 18, they were justified in not seeking the Death Penalty. When the DA's Office contacted the Cosby family they learned that they weren't demanding that the defendant be sentenced to Death. The Cosby Family took the high road and wanted justice to be served and they weren't seeking some type of retribution.

With the Death Penalty issue decided, the DA's Office had to assign a seasoned prosecutor to the Markhasev case. Trial Prosecutors come in three basic categories. First, you have the traditional ones who dress the part and project a confident image. Next, you have the ones who are tough as nails, unsympathetic to the accused. And finally, there are the low key, 'down to earth', type of prosecutors. They could be your next door neighbor who you have learned to trust.

Anne Ingalls fit in the latter category. Anne was 42 years old and had been a prosecutor for 14 years. On a first encounter with Anne, one notices her exceedingly composed demeanor. Her eyes are transfixed on whomever she is conversing with. Her strong suit is that she quietly listens to anyone from a witness to an attorney or even a judge. She is not the type who cuts the other person off, but gives them her undivided attention. After the other person fully expresses themselves, she responds in a calm manner using 'down to earth' language. She never tries to impress anyone with fancy words. She has a unique talent to summarizing complex issues into bite size easily digestible words.

The press became acquainted with her and described her as well-balanced and a well-grounded individual. She did not seek out the news media but she always kept her word. The biggest complaint that the press had about her was the fact that in the courtroom she was hard to hear because of her soft spoken voice. The press's other complaint about her was that she wasn't confrontational enough with witnesses or defendants. Seldom did she revert to shouting at witnesses even when she knew they were lying. She would merely say "Oh, I see" and would paraphrase their answer. Then she made a note to herself to cover that in her Argument at the end of the trial.

As a prosecutor she didn't try to seek out publicity cases to advance her career in the DA's Office. Some attorneys like to 'cherry pick' their cases in order to have a more impressive conviction rate. But her supervisors realized that she could get the job done without complaining and creating any theatrics in the Office. Beside her good nature, she was quickly recognized for her strong litigation skills. Just like cream which always rises to the top no matter what. She didn't take long to rise to the Major Crimes Division. The DA's Office trusted her with some of the toughest cases and she didn't blink and took them on to successful conclusions.

The Defense Attorney was Henry Hall who was from the Alternate Public Defenders Office. His office was set up to handle conflict cases. Since key witnesses in the DA's case had or were being represented by the Public Defender's Office, a conflict was declared and the Alternate Public Defender had to supply a criminal defense attorney for Mikhail. One of the most experienced attorneys in that Office was Henry Hall, who was 47 years old and had numerous capital murder cases under his belt. He was a very thorough attorney who was relatively low-keyed compared to some of the more Perry Mason types.

Jury selection can be the key point in many trials. No question the Mikhail case was going to be a challenging case for both sides. The Defense had their Aces up their sleeves in that they had a lot of ammunition to shoot down many of the prosecution witnesses who had criminal records. The Defense knew they would have trouble putting the defendant on the witness stand since once he opened his mouth, the jury would lose any sympathy for him which they might have since he was a teenager. He fit the definition of a young PUNK. The Defense knew they needed jurors who would be willing to find a Reasonable Doubt with the DA's evidence.

Who makes the best Defense jurors and who would be more favorable for the prosecution? The Defense's spin on the case was that it was Eli Z who committed the shooting. The Defense needed jurors like teachers and engineers who want the evidence to easily add up like a formula. They tend to over analyze the facts and become confused in applying the Reasonable Doubt standard. The Defense would do better with younger jurors who could identify with and understand teenagers running around to buy drugs late at night.

The prosecution was looking for older jurors who were 'stake holders' in the community; people who were fearful of being a victim of a robbery. Basically, the DA would prefer jurors who fit the mold as a typical 'law and order' proponent. Since the case was being tried in the Santa Monica Courthouse, the jurors tend to be more upscale as far as income and more community minded.

The issue of the race card almost always raises its ugly head in mixed racial cases like this one where the defendant and victim were of different races. However, this case was the opposite of the usual since in most cases the defendant is black and the victim is white. Needless to say, in most cases the Defense is trying to get as many minorities on its jury. Since the Cosby family was present in the courtroom, the Defense had to rethink the proposition that minority jurors are always more sympathetic to minority defendants.

The bottom line was the jury that was finally accepted consisted of six women and six men, with four African Americans. Neither side finished up with the jurors they were hoping for, but at least the jurors selected seemed acceptable to both sides.

The jury selection process occurred in rapid succession since Judge David Perez was known as a judge who ran a tight ship. He didn't like to waste the court's time especially during jury selection with what he thought was irrelevant questioning of the jurors by the attorneys. All attorneys knew they needed to be well prepared when trying a case in his court. He was the type of judge prosecutors liked to try a case in his court since everything moved along in an orderly fashion. The only downside is when you have witnesses who don't show up on time; that can be a problem for the DA. This can be exasperating since a prosecutor couldn't afford to be caught without some witness to put on the stand. This made the prosecutor's job most challenging since this case was made up of a number of flakey witnesses.

Since the shooting occurred below Mulholland Drive, the proper judicial district for trial was the old Santa Monica Courthouse. It is located on a slight knoll that faces the Pacific Ocean. From its wide front doors you merely walk three blocks and you are on the sunny beach under the legendary Santa Monica pier. So many judges, prosecutors, and public defenders strive to be assigned to this old courthouse.

It was built in the 1950's and has seen its share of celebrity cases pass through its doors. It is constructed of concrete block walls which gives the visitor a cold, musty feeling. This is especially true in Judge Perez windowless courtroom number 202 with its old fashion fluorescent tubing lighting.

As the time drew near for the first day of trial, members of the Cosby family assembled in one of the row of seats in the spectator's section. There was Ennis' mother, Camille Cosby, age 54, and she was surrounded by Ennis' sisters: Erika 33, Erinn 31, Ensa 15, and Evin 21. All their names started with "E" which stood for EXCELLENCE.

Later on during the trial, Bill Cosby appeared in the spectator section with his family. One of the days he was present there was a short court recess so he had a chance to look directly at Mikhail Markhasev. As Mikhail turned his head to look at the spectators, the two men's eyes met. Each became fixated at staring at the other. Mikhail tried to maintain his smirky smile while glaring at Bill Cosby. The two were locked in a glance that could kill. After several moments, Mikhail flinched first and spun around in his seat and tried to avoid looking at the Cosby family.

It was time for the Opening Statement which commenced with the prosecutor. Anne Ingalls approached the jury and with her typical low key style greeted the jurors with a "hi" and a warm smile. Anne knew she had the most difficult task of explaining the facts of the case without knowing exactly what she would be able to prove. The case could end in a mistrial if she talked about a witness who she couldn't produce or who changes their story. She knew she was on solid ground while explaining what Stephanie C would be testifying to. Stephanie was a reliable witness even though she couldn't identify Mikhail as the shooter.

Anne had to carefully maneuver through what she hoped her other witnesses would testify to. She knew that the witnesses were in deadly fear of retaliation from Mikhail's gang members. Witnesses like Chris So and Michael Chang could be great witnesses who could easily convict Mikhail. Yet, both were scared to death, so would they freeze up on the stand? Anne had her concerns how strong would Eli and Sara be? They could place Mikhail at the crime scene committing the attempted robbery. Nonetheless, both Eli and Sara had burglary charges pending against them on another unrelated crime. They were scared if they testified against Mikhail they would be viewed as snitches. That could be deadly for them if they were convicted of the burglary charges and sentenced to jail.

Anne could explain to the jury that the gun was found in a park by the police and she had experts who could say that it was positively identified as the murder weapon. She also felt she could talk about Gabe D who saw Mikhail's group leave his place shortly before the shooting. She was hopeful that Isaac B would testify that Mikhail came over to his girlfriend's place and he and Eli were glued to the TV listening to the news regarding the shooting of Ennis. The prosecution's Opening Statement was couched in generalities only to give the jury a basic understanding of the facts of the case with the details to be disclosed later during the trial.

Defense attorney Hall was pleased to have the opportunity to tell the jurors of the Defense's version of the facts. He explained the defendant, Markhasev, was with Eli Z and Sara P in the car and they were driving around looking for some friends. That was when Eli stopped the car and got out and shot Ennis Cosby. He jumped back in the car and drove to a place where Eli hid the murder weapon. If his client, Mikhail, was guilty of anything, it was no more than his associating with a robber, Eli, and maybe helping him get rid of the gun. Hall was confident that he would be able to extract testimony from Eli and Sara to get them to paint a picture that they were the real criminals.

CHAPTER 13

PROSECUTION WITNESSES

Seventeen months had passed since Ennis Cosby had been killed. Twelve jurors filed into the courtroom ready to hear the first witnesses in the trial of Mikhail Markhasev. They took their respective seats in the jury box trying to orientate themselves to their new surroundings for the next two and a half weeks. The judge asked the prosecutor, Anne Ingalls, to start calling her witnesses. In a relaxed fashion, which is so indicative of Anne, she said, "The People wish to call Stephanie C." The tension in the courtroom was felt by all those present and Anne knew she needed to put this witness at ease. She knew that the news media had been hounding Stephanie trying to learn more about her background. The prosecutor couldn't afford to have this witness choke up in front of the jurors.

Anne tried to diminish the pressure as much as possible by trying to have Stephanie direct her attention to her and not at all the media representatives in the audience staring at her. For all these months, Stephanie had been in hiding and carefully avoided speaking to the media. The tabloids had harassed her trying to obtain a story of what happened at the crime scene. The media offered her a small fortune if she would tell all. She had taken the high road and not given any media interviews and that was why her testimony was creating so much attention.

The prosecutor had Stephanie explain the reason for meeting with Ennis. The two had met at separate parties occurring at the same time at the Chateau Marmont Hotel on Sunset Strip. Ennis confided in Miss C that he had recently broken up with his girlfriend and was sharing his disappointment with her. Stephanie was with a date but she didn't mind talking to young Ennis. They exchanged phone numbers and later on two other occasions he called her up and they conversed. Then, on January 16th he called again, and this time he wanted to meet with her personally. She indicated in court that she spent the evening at home after visiting her sister earlier in the day. She indicated she was home and invited him to come over to talk. In her testimony she related that a short time later he called again indicating he had a flat tire and would be late. Since it was a dreary rainy night, she said that she insisted on going to help him in any way possible.

She described to the jury what she saw when she arrived. She indicated that it was slightly after 1:00 a.m. and Ennis appeared to be leaning over the front left tire of his Mercedes fixing a flat tire. When she pulled up, Ennis came over to her and she asked how she could help. The weather was freezing cold with an intermittent drizzle. Ennis came over and leaned down and hugged me and said, "Hello, friend". She told him, "I can't believe you're doing this." Then he said, "I like working on cars." He asked her to move her car slightly so its headlights could illuminate Ennis' car. She complied and waited inside her car with the engine running so the car heater kept the car warm. Then she testified a young white male in a light colored watch cap appeared. He rapped on the driver's side window and ordered, "Open the door or I'll shoot you".

She related to the jury that she was terrified and she immediately locked the doors and sped away proceeding up Skirball Drive to Mulholland Drive. She told the jury that she was concerned for Ennis so she made an immediate "U" turn and slowly drove back down Skirball Drive noticing a person run off to the side to another car, jumped in, and then it sped off. As she turned her head to look for Ennis, she saw him lying in a pool of blood next to the driver's door.

The next issue the prosecution asked about was the description of the suspect. She indicated that she told the police that the young man had sharp features and a smooth complexion. She was shown a police composite sketch and asked if she helped to make it. She indicated that a forensic artist had made it at her direction. During the cross-examination Markhasev's attorney harped on the fact that she could not identify the defendant in a police line-up. She had to admit that she had identified someone else as the shooter and not the defendant.

The prosecution assessment of Stephanie C's testimony was that she came across as a credible witness but she certainly couldn't place Mikhail at the crime scene. That was when Gabe D was called as the next witness. He said that around 12:20 a.m. Markhasev and his friend, Eli Z, with Eli's girlfriend had left his house which is located two miles from the crime scene. Although this witness' testimony didn't place Markhasev at the crime scene, at least it placed him within two miles shortly before the shooting.

Another witness who the prosecution called was Isaac, a friend of Markhasev. He testified that Markhasev arrived at his girlfriend's house at 2:00 a.m. and he and Eli

Z were glued to the TV news programs. They were still watching when Isaac left for work later in the morning.

Then the prosecution started calling the police witnesses. The prosecutor lead off with Detective John Garcia who identified certain letters allegedly written by Markhasev while in jail to his a fellow gang member, David G, who was a jailhouse informant for the police. Some of the letters had been found in the trash at the home of David's girlfriend. Other letters were given by Markhasev to a jailer, which were to be mailed, but were confiscated by the jailer and turned over to the detectives.

A Handwriting expert was called and testified that the writing showed normal variations, but on the whole, individual characters were similar to those in other correspondence written by Mikhail. One of these letters stated "This was a Robbery gone Bad". Also it stated that, "I started out to rob a connection and obviously found something else". This was signed by the name "Pee-wee" which was described as Markhasev's moniker.

Markhasev's public defender tried to make it appear that someone else had faked the letters and that Markhasev had not written them. He inferred that it was the jailhouse informant who had fabricated all the letters.

Then the detective who was present when the gun was found testified to the discovery of the weapon. That witness was followed by the Ballistics expert who was able to testify that the gun that was found matched the bullet fragment slug removed from Ennis' head.

The next witness for the prosecution was the Coroner/Medical Examiner who testified during the autopsy of Ennis Cosby, that a bullet slug was removed from his head. He also testified that the cause of death was the one shot to the head.

Other witnesses from the crime lab testified that they had examined the watch cap and found a human hair which was removed. This hair was analyzed for its DNA and the results matched the DNA of Mikhail Markhasev.

Up to this time the prosecution had basically relied on Circumstantial Evidence to make their case that Markhasev was the shooter. All the testimony regarding the gun and the hair in the watch cap relied on the prosecution using Chris So and Michael Chang to connect that gun to Markhasev. Without their testimony, the prosecution basically had no case since they couldn't tie Mikhail to the shooting or the crime scene.

CHAPTER 14 KEY WITNESSES CHRIS SO AND MICHAEL CHANG

Anne Ingalls was struggling with what evidence she had available to prove the case because of compounding witness problems. In the afternoon she was finishing up with one of her last police witnesses. She leaned over to her Witness Coordinator and said, "Contact Chris So and get him into court for tomorrow." She knew that she would be out of witnesses by the next morning and to avoid the wrath of the judge she needed to have a witness ready to testify. The Witness Coordinator had been in constant contact with Mr. So and had allowed him to be placed 'On Call' status. The agreement the DA's Office had made with Mr. So was for him to make himself available to come to court with a two hour notice.

The Witness Coordinator called the number that Mr. So had provided him. However, no one answered the phone. Over the next hour the Witness Coordinator made several more calls without anyone answering. The DA coordinator called a unit in the field and asked that an officer go to Mr. So's address to check to see if Mr. So was there. In less than an hour the unit called back indicating no one was answering the door.

The court session had ended for the day and the Coordinator called Anne and indicated that they had lost contact with Mr. So. Anne in her usual constrained way stated that she needed him in court for tomorrow since she was out of witnesses. She indicated that the judge wasn't going to tolerate a delay. The judge had set a strict schedule for the case since he had assured several jurors who had commitments that they would be finished with their jury service by a certain date.

At that moment in time there was a realization by LAPD and the LADA's Office that they needed to join their resources to find this witness. The success or failure of this Markhasev case depended on them using every tool in their arsenal. There is an old saying that applies to this type of situation and that is, 'you don't want to really know how sausage is made.' Here Anne didn't want to know how Mr. Chris So could be found, but the bottom line was that she needed him in the Santa Monica courtroom first thing in the morning. To this day it isn't known as to all the magic that the two agencies did to try to locate Mr. So. The best explanation was that the DA's Office knew Mr. So's cell phone number. By working with the phone company they were able to triangulate where his cell phone was located.

The incredible part is that they had only a general idea where he was in an apartment house in Orange County. With some good police work they isolated the apartment where he was hiding. No one was more surprised than Mr. So when the police agencies knocked on the door. It is understandable why Mr. So was terrified of Markhasev's gang members. He didn't want to testify even if it meant he wouldn't receive the remaining amount of the $100,000 reward offered by the National Enquirer. He thought his life was worth more than the reward.

These are the tough decisions that prosecutors have to make. Anne knew that she didn't have any chance to get justice in the Ennis Cosby case if Mr. So didn't testify. She certainly didn't want any harm to come to Mr. So but there were others ways of protecting his safety. But first she needed his testimony in court in front of the jury.

When the officers located Mr. So, they asked him why he had not stayed 'On Call' as he had agreed. He explained his fear of testifying against Markhasev. The police told Mr. So that they were taking him into custody under the court authority of a 'Body Attachment'. The officers explained that they would transport him to the Santa Monica court in the morning so he could testify.

That next morning Anne, in her usual unflappable manner, strolled into the courtroom without showing anyone the anguish she had gone through all night long while they were trying to track down the allusive Mr. So. Markhasev and his attorney had no idea what Anne had to do to have Mr. So appear in court. Anne gave the appearance of being calm, cool, and collected. She was the consummate trial attorney who had learned the first lesson of any great litigator which is, **'Never let the jurors see you sweat.'**

What Anne didn't know was how Mr. So was going to react when he was brought into court in the custody of the officers. In order to soften the tension in the courtroom, Anne positioned herself to the side away from the counsel table. In that way, Markhasev couldn't stare at Mr. So and dissuade him from testifying. Would Mr. So clam up and refuse to testify? Would he reluctantly testify in order to earn the rest of the $100,000 reward?

No one really knew how critical the situation had become. If Chris So didn't testify to Mikhail taking him to look for the weapon, the gun and hair with the defendant's DNA would not be admissible in court. The Cosby family was in the courtroom believing justice was being dispensed. It was unknown whether Mikhail was aware of the difficulty in locating Mr. So. The defendant's street gang was attempting to threaten witnesses but nothing could be proven as to how they were going about it.

At the appropriate moment, the judge asked the prosecutor if she had any additional witnesses to call. Anne slowly stood up and stated, "We do your honor, the People would like to call Mr. Chris So to the witness stand." At that moment one of the DA investigators escorted Mr. So into the courtroom. To minimize the eye contact that the witness would have with the defendant, Anne guided him to the witness stand.

She stood near the jury box and started asking questions. She asked some basic questions causing him to look toward her. Immediately she asked about the incident of searching for the gun. He admitted that he was asked by Michael Chang to go with Mikhail to look for a gun in a park like area in North Hollywood. Before searching for the gun, Mikhail was sort of bragging that he was a big dude. He said, "I shot a N----- It's all over the news. I got to hide- this is really big." He explained how panicked Mikhail became when they couldn't find the gun. He testified that Mikhail said, "I got to go back. I got to find that gun."

By this time, Mr. So was making eye contact with Mikhail and his testimony took on a less cooperative attitude. He stated he was afraid for his life, fearing retaliation from Mikhail's gang friends. He admitted that he had contacted the National Enquirer and told them that he knew where the murder weapon might be located. He related to how he went with the police and showed them the general area where they should search for the gun.

Mr. So was asked to look at the composite sketch which Stephanie C had helped create. He was asked if he recognized the person depicted in the sketch and he replied that it looked like the defendant. The prosecution scored no zinger during Mr. So's testimony; however, it had planted a seed that the prosecution could use later in the DA's Argument.

Chris So's testimony wasn't lengthy but was highly crucial for the prosecution. The Defense tried to pin him down on cross-examination. They tried to attack his credibility which this witness didn't care about. The prosecution was pleased that So had been found and testified to the search for the gun. They didn't care if he took some hits by the Defense since he wasn't exactly going to win an award as a stellar citizen of the year. Anne's feeling was the jurors wouldn't have too great of an expectation of the person who was willing to search for a murder weapon. On top of that, he double crossed the murderer by trying to collect on a reward for Mikhail's conviction.

After Mr. So testified, Anne felt that the DA's case had dodged a fatal bullet by finding Mr. So and getting him to testify. Anne wasn't finished yet in that she needed to have Michael Chang testify in court to his role in trying to find the gun for the defendant. Anne thought this would be a piece of cake since Mr. Chang was already in jail on some other criminal matter. She wasn't going to have LAPD and the DA's Office spend time and resources in locating Chang for court since he was already in custody.

Prosecutors learn that 'Murphy's Law' applies just when you think things are going well. Anne called as her next witness Michael Chang. The bailiff went through the custody door and escorted Mr. Chang into the courtroom. Anne knew that Mr. Chang was not looking forward to being a witness. But the question was how hostile could he be to the prosecution's case. If the prosecutor calls a witness and they refuse to testify, the prosecutor can have the judge declare the witness in contempt of court. The penalty for that is a fine or being placed in custody until the witness is willing to testify.

Since Mr. Chang had no money, a fine wasn't going to persuade him to testify. Also, since Mr. Chang was already in custody, the threat of being thrown in jail was meaningless. Anne asked the witness to state his name; however, he refused to answer any questions even to state his name. After considerable dialogue by the prosecutor and the judge to Mr. Chang, it was apparent that he wasn't going to cooperate at all even though Mr. Chang had previously told the police that Mikhail had asked him to find the gun he had hidden. He had related to the police that Mikhail said he had killed a black dude and it was all over the newspapers.

Anne realized that she was not going to get any testimony before the jury as to all the incriminating statements that Mikhail had made to Chang. There was no way she could play the tape recordings of all of Mr. Chang's statements to the police. The reason being, the defendant has a right to have his attorney cross-examine the witness. In this case, if Mr. Chang didn't testify then the defendant's attorney wouldn't have the opportunity to cross-examine him. This was going to have devastating consequences for the prosecution.

Anne, in her most pleasant voice and laced with a slight degree of sarcasm, thanked and excused Mr. Chang. The judge directed the bailiff to remove Mr. Chang from the courtroom by leading him out through the custody door. The Defense was elated with Mr. Chang's refusal to testify. However, Anne hadn't 'fallen off the

Turnip Truck'. She had always been a creative attorney in the courtroom. There were those who might have felt sorry for Anne since it appeared that the carpet had been pulled out from under the prosecution's case.

To everyone's surprise in the court, Anne had a detective bring into court a tape recorder. She put a tape in the recorder and had the detective take the witness stand. She asked him if he was present when Mr. Chang made a secretive phone call to Mikhail who was housed in the Men's Central Jail. The recording was made in the early stages of the case when Mr. Chang was being very cooperative with the police since he didn't want to be charged with Accessory After the fact to Murder. At that time, Mr. Chang was more than willing to 'stiff in' a phone call to Mikhail.

Anne asked the detective if he had the phone conversation tape recorded to which he said that he had. She asked him whose voices were on the tape and he said Mr. Chang and Mikhail Markhasev. The Defense vehemently objected to the playing of the secretive tape recording. Anne claimed it contained an admission by the defendant and was admissible under the exception to the hearsay rule. The judge agreed with the prosecutor that the tape was a mere admission by the defendant and was admissible. The Defense then claimed that the recorded admission was a violation of the defendant's Miranda Rights since he hadn't waived his rights. Anne reminded the court that for Miranda to apply the defendant needed to be in police custody and being **interrogated** by the police. In this incident, no police officer was asking any questions of Mikhail since the secretive phone conversation was between Mr. Chang and Mikhail. The second element of Miranda didn't apply, so the judge ruled that the prosecution could play the taped conversation as long as the detective could identify the two voices on the tape as being Mr. Chang's and Mikhail's voices.

The jury sat spellbound as they listened to the clandestine recorded phone conversation that was laced with vulgarities, street language, drug talk, and conversation about killing a "RAT." While the tape was played, the jurors followed along with a transcript in which they heard an angry Mikhail tell Mr. Chang to "Shut the f--- up" for talking about the gun over the telephone. It was apparent that Mikhail thought that the conversation might be recorded. However, with all the warnings he gave to Chang, Mikhail did say on the tape that he never went back to find the weapon. At the end of the tape, Anne asked the detective if he recognized the voices of the parties on the tapes to which he said they were Mr. Chang calling Mr. Markhasev.

Anne then asked the officer to interpret what was stated on the tape. The detective said that the portion of the tape that stated, "Did you find the strap?" indicates that the word "strap" in gang talk meant "gun." He went on to explain that the police had asked Mr. Chang to stiff in a phone call to Mikhail to see if he would talk about searching for the gun. The pretense of the conversation was whether Mikhail ever found the gun on a later date.

The detective continued to explain that the next part of the tape was Mikhail's voice as follows, "Shut the fuck up. I didn't throw rat shit. I mean, I didn't throw shit, I never went back looking for it." "Hey, Homes with a fucking rat you know you can't do shit. You either kill him or you leave him alone, dog. You know what fucking time it is, baby..." The remainder of the taped conversation consisted of tough guy gang talk.

Anne was pleased that by playing the tape recording provided the corroboration that was needed to allow Mr. So's testimony to remain on the record. Without the statement by the defendant admitting to the gun and the lack of finding it, there wouldn't have been sufficient corroboration to support Mr. So's testimony. The entire case rested on Mr. So's statements that he made about Mikhail and without it the DA had no case. The Mr. Chang fiasco wasn't a pretty scene but Anne had found another way to save the case and legally allow the prosecution to go forward.

However, the unspoken benefit for the prosecution was that the jury got a taste of what Mikhail was really like. Up to this point in the trial, the Defense had decked Mikhail out in a suit and tie making him look like a 'choir boy.' The language he used on the tape recording and his tone of voice spoke volumes to the jurors in that he wasn't really the person that the Defense had dressed him up to be.

The next crucial question was how well would the next two potential witnesses do. They were the other people at the crime scene at the time of the shooting. Eli Z was the driver of the get-a-way car and the driver's girlfriend, Sara, who was also in the vehicle.

CHAPTER 15 TRIAL STRATEGY

The purist would like to believe that in a criminal trial both sides present all the evidence they have and leave it up to an impartial jury to render a just verdict. However, that isn't how the jury system works in the USA. It isn't a level playing field since there are all sorts of legal impediments the attorney has to contend with. A few of the legal concepts are that the prosecutors have to prove their case beyond a reasonable doubt and need a unanimous verdict. The Defense doesn't have to do anything since there isn't any burden for defendant to prove anything. The Defense can sit back and merely attempt to punch holes in the DA's case.

That doesn't mean that the Defense has a perfect cake walk. Many of the jurors have a built-in suspicion of the defendant by the mere fact that he or she have been charged with a crime. Often the defendant doesn't project the type of image of a person that the jurors would invite over for dinner. When it comes to trial, the prosecution witnesses are made up of victims and officers who have the aura of credibility. They evoke a feeling of trustworthiness.

However, this case of the ***People vs. Mikhail Markhasev*** was a major challenge for the prosecution. The witnesses that the prosecutor, Anne Ingalls, had to rely on all had some type of baggage regarding their past. The prosecutor had a dilemma which was to put on a basic case and argue the hell out of it or put on all the prosecution witnesses and let the Defense attorney have a field day of shooting out their legs from under them.

Tracy W was the first person to contact the police about Mikhail leaving Gabe's girlfriend's place around 12:20 a.m.. If that witness would be called as a witness she could be asked about cocaine charges she faced in New Jersey. That would undercut her credibility. It was as though there was a mine field that the prosecution had to maneuver through without being tarred with the claim that they are relying on tainted witnesses. Fortunately for the prosecution, Tracy's testimony wasn't crucial since Anne could use Gabe to testify to the fact that Mikhail, Eli, and Sara left his place around 12:20 a.m..

The prosecution knew they were going to have major credibility issues since both Chris So and Michael Chang had felony convictions that the jury would definitely hear about from the Defense attorney. That was not to mention the fact that the Defense had the Ace card since both Chang and So were going to receive a substantial reward if in fact Mikhail were convicted. The Defense was certainly going to question their credibility since they really had a stake in making sure that Mikhail was convicted.

But the biggest credibility issue involved the possible testimony of Eli Z who was with Mikhail just before and after the shooting. Obviously, his testimony would spell out exactly that Mikhail said he was going to 'Jack' someone. He could describe that Mikhail left with a gun in his hand when he approached Ennis Cosby. He could relate what he saw Mikhail do as far as the attempted robbery. Mikhail also told him where to drive to get rid of the gun and watch cap. Likewise, Eli's girlfriend could basically testify to the same as Eli.

What could be better evidence to convict Mikhail? There couldn't be any witnesses who were more deeply embedded in the case. However, when it came time to testify at the trial, Eli refused to testify claiming his rights under the Fifth Amendment. Anne had to consider long and hard whether to agree to grant immunity to him in order to get him to testify.

However, Anne was a prosecutor with good instincts as well as being an adept poker player. She knew when to 'Hold Them." She could see what cards the Defense had to play. The Defense was setting up the case to make it appear that Eli Z was the real shooter since he was admittedly at the shooting and fit the description of the shooter. If she granted him immunity, the Defense would claim that the DA had made a pack with the devil and in essence, blocked itself from ever prosecuting the real killer of Ennis Cosby who was Eli.

Anne wasn't going to allow the Defense to force her to grant immunity to Eli or his girlfriend, Sara. She knew that the Defense attorney couldn't wait to ask on cross-examination whether Eli and Sara had a felony conviction and whether they were awaiting trial themselves on a burglary charge. Once the jurors heard about Eli's and Sara's background most likely the jurors would not give much weight to their testimony. On top of this, the prosecutor knew that the Defense would try to get in front of the jury the fact that Eli Z was the son of an Israeli mobster convicted of a double murder in 1981. Technically that shouldn't be relevant but it never ceases to amaze prosecutors how the Defense can get such highly prejudicial evidence before the jury.

The only thing that the prosecutor did regarding Eli Z was to have the judge order him to be brought into court so the jury could observe his appearance. As he walked into the courtroom, the jurors could see he was in handcuffs wearing an orange jail jumpsuit. He was instructed to walk up to the jury box and stood there. The judge asked him to turn around twice so all the jurors got a good look at him. Then, without asking him one question, another bailiff escorted him out of the courtroom.

Anne Ingalls made that strategic decision not to call Eli or his girlfriend. The Defense was caught short since they were relying on them testifying. In his Opening Statement, the Defense counsel, Henry Hall, had said that he would prove to the jury that Eli was the real shooter, not Mikhail. This strategic move by the prosecution was a gutty move. Now the prosecution would have to rely on the limited amount of evidence that they were able to elicit in hopes that would be sufficient to convict the defendant.

The Defense attorney, Henry Hall, stated the he was floored that the prosecution had decided against calling Eli Z and Sara P. He had subpoenaed the Defense witnesses to appear later in the week since he thought the testimony of Eli Z and Sara P would take several days. Legally the Defense could try to call either of them as witnesses. However, since they refused to testify unless they received immunity, there was no way the Defense could force them to testify. The Defense doesn't have the power to grant immunity, only the prosecution has that power. The obvious reason is that the prosecution is the only legal agency that has the power to charge people with crimes or the only agency that can agree not to charge someone with a crime.

In reality, the Defense didn't want to call Eli Z or Sara P as witnesses but only wanted to cross-examine them to plant the seed that Eli was the real shooter. This change in the prosecution's strategy really changed the dynamics of the trial. The Defense had committed themselves in their Opening Statement to proving that someone else shot Ennis.

The Defense attorney Hall now realized that they wouldn't have a chance of using Eli Z and Sara P to establish their theory that Eli Z was the real shooter. Attorney Hall quickly changed his approach to a three prong Defense. **First**, he had to rely on the composite sketch to look more like Eli Z than Markhasev. He had to dwell on the fact that Stephanie C had picked out someone else's photo in the photo line-up. His **second** line of Defense was that the alleged letters written by his client were really a forgery from a jailhouse informant. He tried to support that position by the fact that the informant, David G, was a convicted forger. The Defense presented all sorts of evidence to imply that the informant's credibility was in doubt.

The **third** prong involved the tape recorded phone conversation between Markhasev and Chang. Attorney Hall tried to imply that Markhasev was really talking about a different gun than the one used to shoot Ennis. The Defense's hope was to try to muddy up Michael Chang who no one on either side was particularly happy with. The difficulty for the Defense was the fact that the credibility of Chang was not the issue since the words spoken on the tape recording were all that was necessary for the jury to consider.

The Defense, from the very beginning, made no suggestions that the defendant, Markhasev, would take the witness stand to testify that he wasn't involved in the shooting. The Defense attorney realized that Markhasev, who was only 19 years old and a proud gang member, would not ingratiate himself to the jurors. As a result, the Defense didn't call Markhasev to testify so the entire Defense was relatively short with few witnesses and limited documentary evidence.

CHAPTER 16 DA'S ARGUMENT

Now that both sides had finished presenting their witnesses and evidence, it was time to move onto the next stage of the trial which was the Argument phase. Anne, the prosecutor, had her work cut out for her. Her case had been full of surprises from some questionable witnesses. The judge had set the Argument to start first thing on Monday morning. That allowed Anne to return to her downtown office and work with the Trial Support Division in creating an organized persuasive Argument. This meant she had Friday, Saturday, and Sunday to prepare charts and diagrams for her Argument.

On Friday, there was a meeting with Anne to determine the best method of arguing the case to the jury. The question was whether to use a PowerPoint presentation or use posters and charts to explain the evidence to the jurors. Because of the type of case and limited equipment in the old Santa Monica Courthouse, it was quickly decided that the use of posters and charts would be the best method to convey the information to the jury. Anne handed a draft of her ideas to me, the author. Since the case was highly circumstantial, it was important that the jury see how all the evidence fitted together and at the same time, pointing to this defendant.

The first of several versions showed how the testimony of certain witnesses incriminated Mikhail. The second and third versions were too busy with so much information on a standard size poster board. By Saturday it was apparent to the author that the jury had to see all the evidence on one poster to understand the interconnection of all the evidence. Anne smiled and said why don't we use one big gigantic poster board with all the prosecution evidence listed on it.

I, the author, said to Anne, "We can do it but how would you transport such a large poster to the Santa Monica court." Anne responded with total self-assurance. "Leave that to me to work out." That settled the size issue.

(A copy of the DA's Argument chart can be found at the end of this book)

The basis of the poster was to place in the center of the chart a photo of Mikhail with his watch cap on. Then place a dozen arrows containing various statements pointing to the photo of the defendant in the center. In order to fit all the text in, many words were abbreviated like Def. was used for the word 'Defendant'. The top arrow was titled "Matches def's description" with a supporting box stating Stephanie C's Description of the Assailant: Pointy Features, High Cheekbones, Very Pointy Nose, Pale, Young, Thin, and Flawless Complexion. Next to this description box was a copy of the composite prepared by the forensic artist with the help of Stephanie C.

The next arrow was titled "Composite Looks like def". This was supported by a box stating, "Chris So said: Looks just like defendant." This was followed by an arrow with the wording, "Def. is in area after murder". This was supported by a photo of Isaac B and a box stating the following: "Defendant did not return pages;

Defendant showed up unexpectedly at his girlfriend's at 2:00 a.m.; Defendant and Eli glued to TV news".

Further down on the left side of the poster was the arrow stating, "Def. admits murder & robbery". This was supported by a box containing the following: "'LETTERS', Robbery gone bad" followed by "Went to rob a connection, found something else". Underneath the box was a copy of the actual handwritten letters with those statements. Now, on the bottom of the poster were two arrows pointing to the defendant. One arrow said, "Def. brags about Murder while looking for gun". To support that was a photo of Chris So with a box that stated, "I shot a N----- it's all over the news. I got to hide- this is really big". Leads L.A.P.D. to where defendant was looking for .38. That box pointed to photo of the actual Taurus .38 gun with the words "used to shoot Ennis Cosby".

The accompanying arrow was titled "Def. is connected to murder weapon". Below that arrow was the photo of the actual watch cap that the gun was found wrapped in. The box with it stated "HAIR; Hair comparison = Defendant; DNA = defendant".

To continue up the right side of the poster was the evidence regarding Michael Chang. This arrow stated, "Def. admits on tape not finding gun". This was accompanied by a photo of Mr. Chang and the language related to the secret tape recording in which Mikhail stated "Shut the fuck up. I didn't throw rat shit. I mean I didn't find shit. I never went back looking for it..."

The next arrow stated, "Def. is in area of murder". To go along with this was the photo of the witness Gabe D listing his testimony stating, "12:25 a.m. defendant left Gabe's house; Defendant wore 2-tone watch cap"; "Rob a Connection"; "Had a BIG-ASS CANNON". Part of that was related to the last arrow which stated, "Def. is wearing a watch cap". This arrow is supported by the accompanying box stating, "WHITE WATCH CAP; Def. wears watch cap; found at def's house; and Def. likes watch caps".

By the time this gigantic poster was completed it was late Sunday afternoon. It covered all the evidence of the prosecution's case on one poster. Although it may have seemed too busy, it was perfect for Anne's low key style. Everything was on this one poster and the jurors could quickly see how all the evidence was tied together. It was the type of chart jurors can wrap their arms around since everything they had to consider was in front of them.

I, the author, had continually reminded Anne that the poster was four feet by eight feet and would be next to impossible to transport in a car. Anne assured me that she had a hatch back car which she had used many times before to carry wide loads. The gigantic chart looked very impressive and was just what Anne wanted. Two of my paralegals, with myself and Anne, maneuvered this monster poster out of the Trial Support Division on the 17th floor down the elevator in the Criminal Courts Building. She had conveniently parked her hatch back in the parking lot next to the exit to the building.

When we arrived at Anne's car I tried to figure out how this poster was going to squeeze into this two seater car. Anne opened the hatch back and we started sliding the poster in. She was right. The poster did slide in when it was titled on one side. We continued to slowly and carefully move the poster further in. Then we hit the back of the front seats and the poster wouldn't slide any further. I looked in the back and could see three feet of poster still sticking out.

Anne, in her un-phased manner, told the paralegals to push the poster above the seat which they did. I told Anne there was no way she would be able to drive the car.

Her remark to me was, "Don't worry Ron, I will manage". She pulled the hatch back lid down and used some type of bungee cord to secure it. By now it was dark out, on Sunday night, as Anne got into the driver's seat. She started up her car and slowly pulled out of the parking lot. I could see the poster board resting on the top of her head as she barely could look over the dashboard. I was concerned that some LAPD traffic officer would pull her over and give her a ticket for driving with impaired vision.

However, I wasn't concerned for Anne since I knew her husband, Vic, who was a Robbery Homicide LAPD detective, would be able to explain the situation to any traffic officer. As Anne pulled out of the parking lot she hit a rut and the hatch back lid came smashing down on the poster board. She kept driving and I could see a long dent mark on what had been a pristine Argument chart. 'Oh well things happen.'

The next morning Anne was in court and the Judge asked her if the People wished to argue the case. Anne answered with a firm voice, "The People are ready to argue". She walked over to a large easel and placed her gigantic poster on it. Everyone in the courtroom was all eyes gazing at the giant poster sized chart. At one end of the poster it appeared to be bent with a few marks from the lid of the hatch back. However, the news media was so intrigued with it that they didn't notice the blemishes to the poster which occurred on its journey from downtown to Santa Monica courthouse.

Anne made direct eye contact with the jurors stating, "If we were to pull over with a flat tire, do we have a bull's eye on our back for a predator?" She said, "Mikhail's motive was clear. Ennis Cosby had money, a beautiful car, and a watch. The defendant saw an opportunity. He goes up and tries to take property but gets spooked... He shoots the gun and runs away."

Then Anne started like a brain surgeon to meticulously proceed step by step through her giant poster starting with the arrow pointing to Mikhail from Stephanie C. The jurors were glued to every arrow and listened to her explanation of what evidenced supported it. She worked her way around to each arrow and reminded the jurors that it pointed to Mikhail. Each time she backed up each point by going over to the poster and pointing to the box that explained what evidence proved it.

Anne used common sense language in her Argument. She had a way of simplifying things without insulting the intelligence of the jurors. She had been very careful in her Opening Statement to the jury not to over promise what she was going to be able to prove. Anne realized she didn't know for sure if and how her witnesses would testify. She admitted that some of her witnesses had come with some baggage but she put it in perspective. She stressed that even though their credibility could be questioned there was more than enough corroboration to support their testimony.

Although Anne's Argument might be considered short, it was concise and thorough. She hadn't used any hyperbole or at any time pounded her fist on counsel table. It wasn't flashy or over the top. Anne's presentation was like listening to your best friend explain a serious situation to you. She was believable and everything logically added up. At the end of Anne's Argument, she gave the jurors a big sincere smile and thanked them for their attention. At that moment in the courtroom you could hear a pin drop. It was like in church when the sermon ends. Anne quietly turned and sat down, punctuating the silence.

As everyone in the courtroom reflected on what they heard, Judge Perez ended the silence saying, "This would be a good time to take a break".

CHAPTER 17 DEFENSE ARGUMENT

After the court's recess, everyone reassembled in the courtroom. The judge asked the Defense attorney if he wished to make an Argument to which he answered in a strong voice, "Yes." Mr. Hall stood up and approached the jury. He was a tall professional looking man who fit the part of an attorney. He immediately started to pick apart the prosecution's case piece by piece. Starting with his theory that the real killer was Eli Z, who was with Mikhail at the time, he zoomed in on the fact that Stephanie C couldn't identify Mikhail as the killer. He stressed the fact that she identified a totally different person at the line-up.

Then he focused on the composite sketch and pointed to it and asked the jurors who did it look like? His answer was that the composite looked more like Eli Z. The jurors looked at the composite he was holding up and glanced over to Mikhail to make a quick comparison.

Mr. Hall stated that the prosecution was trying to distort the evidence to fit their theory of the crime. He pointed out that there was no evidence placing Mikhail at the crime scene. Since Eli and Sara had not testified and Stephanie couldn't identify, the Defense was correct that there was no witness directly saying they saw him there. The Defense attorney was hitting the weakness in the People's case. He referred to the fact that the prosecution was merely using circumstantial evidence to prove their case.

Next he zeroed in on witness Chris So. He asked the jury how could they believe him? Here was a man who was paid $40,000 by the National Enquirer for interviews and in the end would receive the rest of the $100,000 reward if Mikhail were convicted. Who would have a stronger motive to lie about Mikhail's involvement in order to gain money for himself? The Defense couldn't have a better witness to beat up on in front of the jury. He had been a hostile witness for the prosecution and they had to basically arrest him to bring him to court. Attorney Hall reminded the jury how it was like pulling teeth to get him to testify for the prosecution. The Defense painted a dark picture of Mr. So's testimony but it didn't help support the spin of the facts that Eli Z did it.

Mr. Hall's Argument regarding Mr. So's testimony was hard hitting. He then shifted his attention to Mr. Michael Chang as a prosecution witness. There was no one in the courtroom who had any love or sympathy for Mr. Chang. The Defense could attack him as much as they wanted but the tape that was played for the jury with all the salty gang language spoke for itself. Mikhail's voice could be clearly heard saying he didn't ever find the gun. The jury didn't have to weigh the credibility of Mr. Chang since he was really a non-witness.

It wasn't until the Defense attorney starter to discuss the so called 'jailhouse letters' did he demonstrate so much contempt for the DA's case against his client. He tried to paint David G the jailhouse informant as nothing more than a forger. Mr.

Hall claimed that the letters were made up to curry favor with the police since the informant wanted his sentence reduced. He tried to illustrate how one of the letters contained different styles of handwriting. He told the jury that the letters were all fabricated and they should totally disregard them.

After spending considerable time talking about the letters, the Defense attorney turned his attention to the hair in the watch cap that contained DNA matching Mikhail. This one strand of hair was what the prosecution relied on to connect Mikhail to the murder weapon. How was the Defense going to spin this most incriminating evidence? Mr. Hall floated the suspicions that the hair may have been planted just to get his client convicted of a murder he didn't commit. He said, "Wasn't it strange that no one found that hair in the watch cap until over a year after the shooting. Why did it take the detectives a year to find that one hair?"

The planted hair in the watch cap was a little difficult for the Defense to sell to the jury. But the Defense had a better Argument when discussing the color of the watch cap. Gabe D had said that Mikhail was wearing a two tone watch cap while Stephanie said it was a light color watch cap. When the gun was found in a watch cap it turned out to be an all-black watch cap. The Defense certainly questioned whether the witnesses' were correct in their description and if they were in error, then maybe they were mistaken about other facts they had testified to.

The Defense attorney Hall acknowledged when finishing up his Argument that he had not delivered on his promise he made in his Opening Statement when he told the jurors that he would prove it was Mr. Z who pulled the trigger. "Now I can't prove to you, based on the evidence that has been presented, that Eli Z committed this crime." However, he reminded the jury of the following, "But when you look at the composite sketch based on a description by Ms. C, it more closely resembled Mr. Z than Mr. Mikhail." This concluded the Defense's Argument.

CHAPTER 18 RESULTS OF TRIAL

When the Defense attorney finished his Argument, he walked over to sit down at the counsel table. Some of the jurors and members of the news media had a puzzled look on their faces. Many seemed to have some 'Doubts' about the People's case. The news media had been expressing self-doubts ever since Anne had not called Eli Z to testify. There was an undercurrent that the prosecution had made a fatal mistake in not granting immunity to Eli Z so the jurors could hear his rendition as to what happened at the crime scene.

Anne had nerves of steel and didn't waiver in her resolve of the defendant's guilt. When the judge asked her if she wanted to make a Rebuttal Argument, she stated with an unequivocal, "Yes". As she rose up out of her chair, she walked confidently toward the jury box. With a stern expression she told the jurors that they had just heard a **"SODDI"** defense. The jurors seemed to recoil in their seats and had a bewildered look as to what she was alluding to. She slowly unraveled the word by saying that when the Defense doesn't have a credible case they resort to using the

"SODDI" defense, meaning **"Some Other Dude Did It."** She related that the Defense wanted to insert Eli Z as the 'Other Dude'.

Then Anne pulled out another chart with Eli Z's photo in the center with eight large arrows pointing to it. Each of the arrows had a large question mark inside. The jurors quickly noticed the similarity between this barren chart and the gigantic poster Anne had used in her Argument. That was when Anne went around each arrow and said where is the evidence that Eli Z did it? Did you hear any witnesses? "No". Was there any documents that showed he did it? "The answer is No."

Years ago in the United States there was a TV Commercial for a fast food company in which an elderly lady would ask, "Where's the BEEF?" Anne was in a similar situation asking, "Where's the evidence to support the 'SODDI' Defense?"

Anne then talked about the issue of trying to rehabilitate witness Chris So. She showed how he was frightened to testify against Mikhail because of his gang contacts. She showed how Mr. So was not the perfect witness but did his testimony add up? When it came to finding the gun, his information was right on target since the gun was found in the general area where Mikhail had told So where he had hidden the gun. Anne tried to explain to the jurors that they didn't have to like Mr. So as a person, but consider whether he was lying about the gun? She answered with a resounding "No".

Anne then addressed the issue regarding the Defense's claim that the letters were forgeries. She had to be very careful how she approached this subject. She couldn't make any comment about the fact that the defendant didn't testify. She couldn't say why the defendant didn't testify that the letters weren't written by him. That would be improper Argument and would be grounds to reverse the case. So Anne asked where was the testimony or the documents that proved that the letters were forgeries? This planted the seed in the minds of the jurors that the mere fact that the Defense attorney claimed the letters were forgeries was not evidence.

As Anne was finishing up with this last point, she could see in the eyes of the jurors that they had heard and seen enough. No more arguing was going to change their minds. She propped her large oversized poster on the easel and said the evidence is all there. In the matter of three minutes, she summarized all the points on the chart. She told the jury that they could see all the evidence in this case and how it all fit together. Then she pointed to the other easel showing the chart with Eli Z's photo in the center with arrows pointing to it containing giant question marks. She said that chart summarized the Defense theory which is not supported by one iota of evidence.

She finished by saying that there was only one chart that was supported by evidence and that was the big poster that had all the evidence pointing to the defendant. Just before sitting down she firmly said, "The evidence proves that the defendant is guilty of first degree murder and attempted robbery".

The courtroom fell quiet until the judge cleared his throat and announced he was about to read the jury instructions. Several members from the news media scampered out of the courtroom before the judge started reading the tedious but important jury instructions. Those reporters were off to call in their stories to their newspapers or others grabbed their handy microphones to go on air to explain to the public what they had just heard in court.

Those who weren't lucky enough to escape before the bailiff locked the doors had to obediently sit through 20 minutes of jury instructions read in the monotone voice of a judge. It appeared that the jurors were anxious to reach the end of the instruction. They seemed ready to start their deliberation. The bailiff escorted them to the jury room to start their discussions. No one could possibly know how long it would take them to arrive at a verdict.

Many of the court watchers were ready for a long session of waiting. Often there are hours of 'Read Back' in which the court reporter reads back various witnesses' testimony. Within the same day the jury buzzed indicating they had reached a verdict. Immediately, the court notified the attorneys involved and contact was made with the media. The jury had been deliberating for a mere six hours. A quick verdict is interpreted as a likely win for the Defense. The reasoning is that there are so many additional sets of verdict forms the jury must go through if they decide to convict.

The parties were given two hours to reassemble for the reading of the verdict. The prosecution notified the Cosby family of the announcement of the verdict. Likewise, the Defense attorney agreed to notify Mikhail's relatives regarding the reading of the verdict. The appointed time arrived and everyone was in their respective seats. The defendant's mother and relatives were nowhere to be seen but it was expected they wanted to be present. The judge entered the courtroom and took his seat. He looked down at the two attorneys and asked if they were ready and both announced they were. The judge ordered the court clerk to call in the jury. Within several minutes the first juror appeared and the others followed to their respective assigned seats.

The judge turned to the jury and asked the foreperson if they had reached a verdict to which the person indicated they had. The judge instructed that the verdict forms be handed to the bailiff to be passed to him for review. Slowly the judge looked over each verdict form to make sure they were filled out correctly. Then he handed them to the court clerk to read them out loud in the courtroom.

This is the high moment when the courtroom clerk is the center of attention and everyone has to listen to her, or in some cases, him. This seems a peculiar tradition in the California courts where the clerk, not the judge or jury foreperson, reads the verdict. The courtroom was totally filled with spectators, even other judges and clerks were poking their heads in to hear the reading of the verdict. The courtroom fell into a deep silence and every ear was leaning in the clerk's direction to hear her utter the verdict.

Court clerks seem to sense the enormous power they have at that particular moment. She cleared her throat and with a strong voice announced that the jury had found Mikhail Markhasev guilty of first degree murder and guilty of attempted robbery. The courtroom experienced an emotional charge as the Cosby family burst into tears. The sisters of Ennis began hugging each other.

The judge tried to maintain some decorum but quickly announced the date for sentencing and then thanked the jurors for preforming their civic duty and excused them from the case. As the judge departed, the jurors in single file walked passed the Cosby family in their emotional moment. Several of the jurors went over to Ennis's mother, Camilla, and hugged her and the sisters. It seemed there wasn't a dry eye in the courtroom except for Mikhail who stood up and with a big smirk turned his head defiantly and was led into custody.

After the jurors had left, Anne had collected all her papers and files and started to walk out of the courtroom when the Cosby family came up to her and hugged her. They thanked and praised the dignified way she had tried the case. Anne tried to find the words she felt for the families' loss. Words seemed to be inadequate to convey to the family what a great lost for them although this was supposedly a moment of victory. Yes, this was a big win for the Cosby family and the DA's Office but no one was in the mood to celebrate.

Anne was hoping this verdict would provide some closure for the family. She knew it would not bring back Ennis who was so dearly loved by his family and everyone he ever came in contact with. After the last hug, Anne knew it was time to keep her promise that she would talk to the news media who were huddled outside waiting for her to exit the courtroom.

As Anne left the courtroom she could see the Defense attorney giving an interview to the media. He blamed the media for his client's conviction. A reporter asked him how the defendant felt about being convicted. In a sarcastic response he said, "He's going to spend the rest of his life in prison...He's 19 years old and it doesn't take a rocket scientist to figure out how he feels about that." It was more than apparent that the Defense attorney was unhappy with the jury verdict.

When the media noticed Anne standing outside the court door they left the Defense attorney and placed their microphones in Anne's direction. Questions came from right and left but Anne wanted to address the answer the Defense had made. She said, "I think Mikhail Markhasev convicted Mikhail Markhasev and not the media." "I think the dignity and the integrity of the Cosby family emanated throughout the whole proceedings."

Anne knew the media would question her about not calling Eli Z and Sara P. When the questions came up she avoided being drawn into the debate. Anne thanked the media and excused herself since she needed to make phone calls to the downtown head office.

February 5, 1999 was set for sentencing. On that day, Mikhail's attorney argued a motion for a New Trial. He claimed that Mikhail didn't receive a fair trial since the six letters used by the prosecution were forgeries. He alleged that an informant had been responsible for making up the letters in order to gain favor with the authorities. One of the letters suggested the Mikhail went to Bel-Air on the night of the shooting to rob a drug dealer. The wording in the letter was "I went to rob a connection and obviously found something else."

The judge listened to the Defense argument and indicated that he wasn't going to find that the letters were a forgery. However, he ruled that there was enough substantial evidence without the letters to support the jury's verdict. The judge then sentenced Mikhail Markhasev to a life sentence without the possibility of parole.

As Mikhail was taken away in his jail jumpsuit he made his last defiant jester to the world by raising his handcuffed hands and gave 'the finger' to the media. Photographers snapped pictures of his jester which ended up on the front page of newspapers around the world. Was this a PUNK kid who wanted to show contempt for the world? Or was it a 19 year old who had just realized he had fucked up his life since he was going to live forever and ever in prison.

The irony in the case came a year later. Markhasev, with his appellate attorney, filed a lengthy appeal. They pointed out all the possible errors Mikhail's trial attorney had made. They complained that the wrong jury instructions were given. There were claims of police and prosecutor misconduct. All the typical claims were made. No one knows how the appellate courts would rule. But in cases involving young defendants, the appellate courts may be a little more sympathetic. In other words, Mikhail had a good chance that some appellate justices would try to find grounds to reverse his conviction.

Out of nowhere came a letter to the appellate court stating that Mikhail wanted to abandon his appeal. He wrote in his handwriting, "I am Guilty and I want to do the right thing... I want to apologize to the victim's family..." This surprised everyone, especially his appellate attorney. Here he was relinquishing any chance of ever being released from prison. Why did he do this? Did he get religion? Was this a case of genuine remorse? Most likely we will never know. All we know for certain was that two young men's lives were forever changed when that .38 Taurus revolver was fired just off of Mulholland Drive on that dark misty morning of January 16, 1997.

The following graphic page shows the chart that the prosecution used in its argument to the jury.

Graphics 1

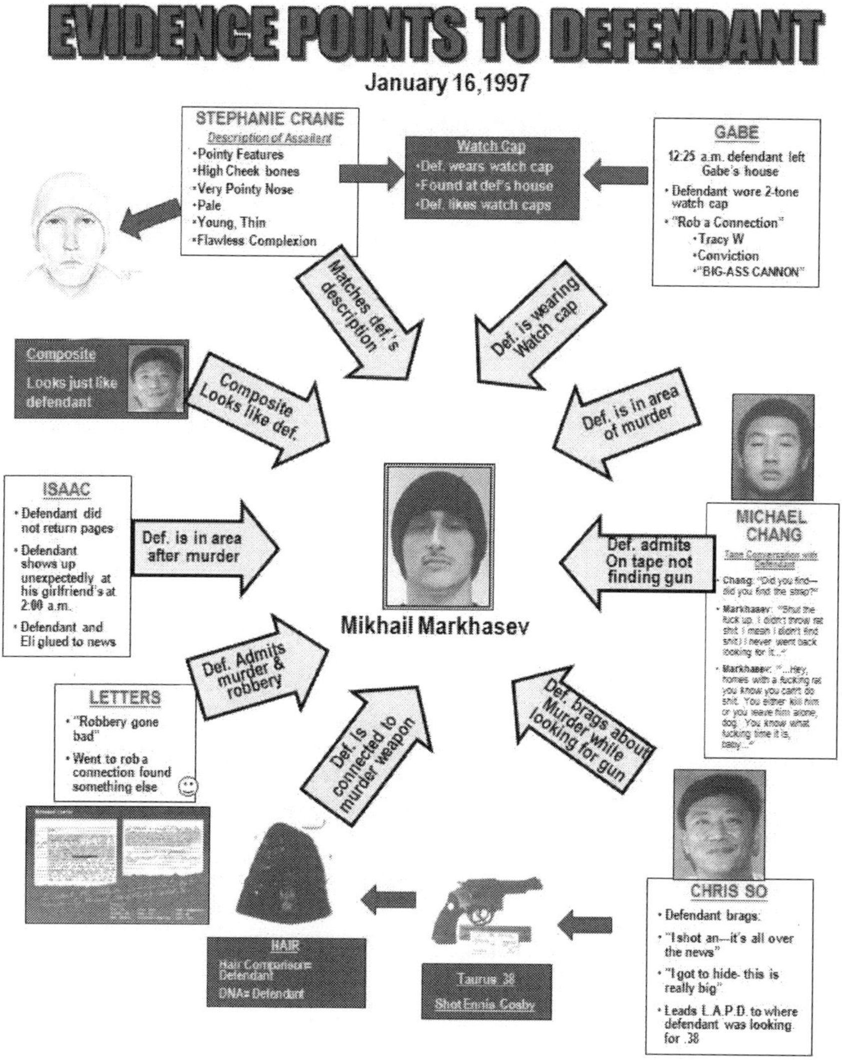
EVIDENCE POINTS TO DEFENDANT
January 16,1997
STEPHANIE CRANE
Description of Assailant
•Pointy Features
•High Cheek bones
•Very Pointy Nose
•Pale
•Young, Thin
•Flawless Complexion
Watch Cap
•Def. wears watch cap
•Found at def's house
•Def. likes watch caps
GABE
12:25 a.m. defendant left Gabe's house
• Defendant wore 2-tone watch cap
• "Rob a Connection"
•Tracy W
•Conviction
•"BIG-ASS CANNON"
Matches def.'s description
Def. is wearing Watch cap
Composite
Looks just like defendant
Composite Looks like def.
Def. is in area of murder
ISAAC
• Defendant did not return pages
• Defendant shows up unexpectedly at his girlfriend's at 2:00 a.m.
• Defendant and Eli glued to news
Def. is in area after murder
Def. admits On tape not finding gun
MICHAEL CHANG
Mikhail Markhasev
Def. Admits murder & robbery
LETTERS
• "Robbery gone bad"
• Went to rob a connection found something else
Def. is connected to murder weapon
Def. brags about Murder while looking for gun
HAIR
Hair Comparison= Defendant
DNA= Defendant
Taurus 38
Shot Ennis Cosby
CHRIS SO
• Defendant brags:
• "I shot an—it's all over the news"
• "I got to hide- this is really big"
• Leads L.A.P.D. to where defendant was looking for .38

CHAPTER 19 LIFE OF BILL COSBY

It would be an understatement that Bill Cosby is an interesting character. He would truly fit in the section of the old Reader's Digest, 'The Most Interesting Person' category. What is also remarkable about him is how long he had endured in the public spotlight. He has been highly revered by many and highly maligned by others. He definitely is not a one dimensional person. He most likely wouldn't quite make sainthood as did Mother Theresa. Mr. Barack Obama wouldn't have become the president of the USA if it wasn't for what Bill Cosby had done in changing a country's perception of blacks during the 80'sand 90's.

Let's examine Bill Cosby starting from his roots. He was born July 12, 1937, in Philadelphia. Academics wasn't his strong aptitude so he dropped out of school in the 10th grade. He was a teenager who lacked direction and discipline until he went into the Navy. There he excelled to the structure of the military and eventually earned his High School diploma. After the Navy, he wanted to give higher education a try and he enrolled in Temple University in 1961. Again he grew bored or distracted to the point he dropped out of college in his sophomore year.

Bill had an outgoing personality but had a natural gift of making people laugh. Somehow he possessed a 'funny-bone' that was the result of the manner in which he saw the world. He could take any situation and find the humor in it. His unusual talent of being funny led him into doing 'Stand Up Comedy'. He soon learned what it took to make audiences laugh. He watched others and noticed that certain topics were inherently fertile fields for comedy. He earned the reputation of being an all-around comedian.

In 1965 he tried his luck working in television. Within a short time he was co-starring in the TV series "I Spy" with Robert Culp. The show became a colossal success with a certain chemistry between these two co-stars, which involved a detective dual who got themselves mixed up in the zaniest situations. For three seasons the TV audience laughed at a white guy and a black guy working as partners fighting crime.

By 1969, Bill's popularity had risen and the network gave him the opportunity to star in his own TV series, "The Bill Cosby Show", which was moderately successful but canceled after two years. Then by 1972 he had a newfangled hit in "Fat Albert & the Cosby Kids" which appealed to both children and adults. This series lasted until 1984 when he debuted his most successful TV show ever titled, "The Cosby Show." This series continued into 1992 and was acclaimed to be the most significant show to change American's thinking about African-Americans.

The show revolved around the daily lives of a Black married couple and their five children. The mother was an attorney and the father was a physician. What the show illustrated was how similar the problems and rewards are for all families no matter their race or cultural background. As a TV series, it addressed various issues that needed discussion and did it in a non-threatening manner.

The basic format of the program copied Bill Cosby's real family which consisted of one son and four daughters. Needless to say, "The Bill Cosby" TV show received an endless number of awards. In 1994 the program was inducted into the Academy of Television Arts & Science Hall of Fame. Bill Cosby received over $300 million from syndication rights. For eight seasons it was a big success and the American audience watched as the children in the program grew up before their very eyes.

Throughout all the triumph of "The Cosby Show," Bill Cosby was doing commercials for so many companies it seemed like he was always popping up on everyone's TV screen in their living room as a pitchman for Jell-O, Kodak, Del Monte, as well as Ford Motor Corporation.

Bill Cosby was a very busy man in the 80's and 90's. His family was vital to him and he tried to be involved in his children's lives. However, his busy schedule saw him traveling all over the country. His wife, Camille, had to be the frontline in caring for the children and all their needs in growing up. However, the death of his son Ennis had a profound impact on Bill Cosby's life.

It was hard for him to adapt to the roll of being a father of a murder victim. In an interview after the tragedy he said, "I am a humorist and I'm to be funny. I don't want to establish myself as a tragic figure, though I loved my son deeply." After a short time for grieving for the loss of Ennis, Bill was back on the road making appearances. His only comment was that he thanked everyone for their prayers and support. Then it was Showtime and he was off telling his folksy jokes.

He privately wanted to honor his son so he established a fund to help needy young people. The charity was called 'Hello Friend, Ennis Cosby Foundation' since that was his son's greeting line when he met others. Bill wanted something positive to come out of his son's tragic death.

If the death of his son wasn't bad enough, his life was infected with scandals that struck at the core of his image as a family man. A woman claimed to be his illegitimate daughter. Her name was Autumn Jackson and she claimed she was going to reveal to the public that Bill Cosby had an illicit affair with her mother. She tried to extort money from Bill Cosby and his family. The entire situation turned ugly and resulted in his so called 'Love Child' being convicted of attempted extortion.

Years later, more women came forth claiming that he had sexual relations with them. These women made all sorts of insinuations that he had plied them with alcohol and drugs to gain their consent. What was peculiar about these allegations was they occurred some 20 to 30 years earlier. These women claimed that no one would listen to them when the incidents occurred so that was the reason they waited to speak up. Several women's groups supported these women in attacking Bill Cosby.

Eventually a deposition was unsealed by a judge in July of 2015, which showed that Mr. Cosby had received Quaaludes to give to women he intended to have sex with. His words were, "She meets me back stage. I give her Quaaludes. We then have sex." As a result of this crusade against Bill Cosby, his career and reputation have forever been denigrated. Ironically, the tabloids who had been the ones who had helped solve the Ennis Cosby case were the same ones that years later castigated his father, Bill Cosby for his deceptive ways to have sex with women.

On June 5, 2017, the trial began in Philadelphia where a female school official was invited to the Cosby estate. There she met with Bill Cosby who gave her several pills that knocked her out. While she was unconscious he sexual violated her. All of this occurred in 2004, many years before the criminal charges were filed against him. At the trial the victim was cross-examined by Cosby's attorney asking her why she had told different stories as to what happened. She tried to explain the reasons for all the inconsistences. The prosecution introduced Cosby's statement he had given at the earlier deposition where Cosby admitted that he had given women drugs so he could have sex with them.

During the trial Cosby didn't take the witness stand. It would seem to be an open and shut case against him. However, Cosby's attorney argued to the jury that Cosby had sex with the victim but it was entirely consensual. The jurors listened to both sides Argument after which they started deliberating. Almost immediately the jury informed the judge that they were deadlocked. The judge continued to have the jurors deliberate. Finally on Saturday morning the jury came back and said that they were hopelessly deadlocked at which time the judge declared a mistrial. After excusing the jurors, the judge reset the matter for a second trial within four months.

In April of 2018, the retrial began and the victim Andrea Constand testified how she was drugged and sexually assaulted by Cosby. Again, he did not testify and his Defense claimed that it was a matter of consensual sex. However, times had changed and this was the first trial after the #Me Too movement began six months earlier. This time the jury had no difficulty finding the 80-year-old Cosby guilty of three counts of sexual assault.

WHY IS MULHOLLAND DRIVE SO WELL KNOWN? WHAT'S THE HISTORY OF THIS HILLY ROAD ON TOP OF LOS ANGELES?

CHAPTER 20

BACKGROUND OF MULHOLLAND DRIVE

Back in 1924 a group of land developers wanted to construct a road that would run along the crest of the Santa Monica Mountains and Hollywood Hills. Around that time the motion picture industry was evolving in Hollywood. The movie stars and film producers wanted to impress others by the opulence of their residential estates. Size matters in Hollywood but most of all height matters even more. In other words, the higher you live up the hill is indicative to your level of success in the eyes of others.

For real estate developers they could see that more money could be made if they created view lots on top of the Hollywood Hills. So a two lane road was carved out along the ridge crest of the Santa Monica Mountains. This roadway would permit the complete development of this prime real estate. The houses built along this road would be the ultimate way to display to others ones accomplishments and achievement.

One of the developments was called **'HOLLYWOODLAND'** and is remembered by the fact that it constructed a huge sign across the hillside. (These days there would be an environmental study that would object to any such commercial scaring of the pristine Hollywood Hills and permission for such a sign would be denied). As time went by, the wooden sign fell into disrepair. The last four letters **(LAND)** were crumbling and tattered and the civic leaders of Hollywood decided to repair the letters '**HOLLYWOOD**' but tear down the' **'LAND'** part.

The HOLLYWOOD sign has become one of the legendary landmarks recognized internationally. Most people think of Hollywood as the Entertainment Capital of the World. In 2014 when a building developer was in the process of purchasing the land on which the sign is located, there was community outcry. The Hollywood residents and business owners demanded the city of Los Angeles purchase the property. The historic preservation group jumped in demanding that the sign be preserved. Then there were environmental groups who claimed the sign was a blight on the community and wanted it torn down. After heated debates, the bottom line was that the HOLLYWOOD sign should be preserved and it has been reinforced with steel so it can last forever as the symbol for Tinsel Town.

When the road that became Mulholland Drive was completed, it started at the Cahuenga Pass on the Eastside and continues to the 405 Freeway and extends to the Ventura County line. If one were to travel the full length of it that would total 21 miles. However, there are sections of the road that are listed as 'Dirt Mulholland' which have been closed off to motor vehicle traffic since it weaves its way through the Santa Monica Hills Conservancy Park. Further west the road becomes more confusing. One section of it continues as Mulholland **Drive** and ends at the Ventura

101 Freeway. But the main portion of the road takes on a different designation by being called Mulholland **Highway** and ending near the Malibu Canyon Road.

The origin of the road's name 'Mulholland' comes from the distant realm of Ireland. The road acquired its name from a famous albeit controversial pioneer of Los Angeles by the name of **William Mulholland**. His claim to fame was he was the visionary who brought water to the arid community of Los Angeles. In 1913 he engineered and built the Los Angeles Aqueduct which brought the abundant water from the Eastern Sierra Mountains to the city of Los Angeles some 233 miles through 164 tunnels and miles of channels and pipes.

The result of all the water from the Aqueduct created the San Fernando Valley. The City of Los Angeles annexed this land which resulted in doubling the size of the city. That is what permitted L.A. to become the second largest city in the U.S.. Eventually, William Mulholland became the chief of the Water Department for the City. So, in 1924, when they were looking for a name for the new road traversing the two parts of Los Angeles, it was understandable why William Mulholland's name was suggested. In 1924, the street signs officially announced this spectacular roadway was christened 'Mulholland Drive.'

Four years later in 1928, William Mulholland's reputation came crashing down on him when the St. Francis Dam, for which he had engineered and certified as being safe, collapsed and created a torrent of water which devastated many communities downstream and ended up taking the lives of over 600 people. This became the worst U.S. civil engineering disaster of the 20th century, which terminated his career and caused him to resign in disgrace.

Many would have liked to change the name of the road from Mulholland; however, it was too late and the name remains even today. What was interesting was the fact that the celebrated movie in 1974, ***Chinatown,*** starring Jack Nicholson and directed by Roman Polanski, was about the Water Wars taking place in the early years of the Los Angeles history. In the movie the character Hollis Mulwray was a depiction of William Mulholland. The movie shows how Mulwray opposed the new dam that the city wanted since Mulwray was fearful that it would be a repeat of what had happened in the St. Frances Dam disaster.

Over the years, movie stars have flocked to buy up the lots along the roadway. In 1941, Errol Flynn bought 11 acres at 7740 Mulholland Drive which was called the **'Mulholland Farm'**. There Flynn built a fashionable house with all the appurtenances of large pool, tennis court, and even a casino. Flynn entertained many starlets and he earned his reputation of 'In Like Flynn' from all the ladies who ended up in his bed.

Later he got himself into some difficulty and left the U.S. for Europe. One of his ex-wives received the Mulholland Farm and eventually it was sold to singer Ricky Nelson, who called it his home for many years.

Over the years, movie stars and entertainment executives have enjoyed living on Mulholland Drive. This is partly due to the spectacular views and the great places to entertain and impress others. Also, it provides more privacy since the lots are more spacious. Psychologically it may make them feel slightly more superior since they are on top of the world looking down on their movie fans below.

Few famous roads have movies made about them. In 2001, a neo-noir mystery film, ***Mulholland Drive***, was written and directed by David Lynch starring Naomi Watts, Laura Harring, and Justin Theroux. The movie doesn't have much to do with the road Mulholland Drive except for an auto accident that occurs there and somehow the victim escapes and is able to find her way down into the city below.

Most people who saw the film didn't gain any information about the famous road. It seemed a film maker was using the famous name **Mulholland Drive** to help promote a less than stellar motion picture.

MURDER IN MARLON BRANDO'S HOUSE

CHAPTER 21 BEFORE THE SHOOTING

May 16, 1990 becomes the key date in our next story. However, perusing history, nothing noteworthy occurred on that date of May 16th. The only claim to fame for that day was that in 1929 the First Academy Awards ceremony was held on that date in Hollywood. The only other significant event to occur on May 16th was that "*Annie Get Your Gun*" opened on Broadway in 1946. However, in 1990, it might have been more appropriate to call it '**Christian Brando Get Your Gun.**' That would better describe what Christian Brando did on that date when he picked up his .45 Caliber semi-automatic handgun and transported it up to his dad's house on Mulholland Drive.

A week before May 16th, Brando's daughter, Cheyenne, her mother and her fiancé Dag Drollet, arrived from Tahiti to stay with Marlon at his Mulholland estate. The purpose of the visit was so Cheyenne could receive better psychiatric therapy in the States. Since Cheyenne was six months pregnant she was given a bedroom for herself. Dag was relegated to camping out in the den using the sofa as his temporary bed.

Christian Brando was living with his girlfriend a short distance away down the hill. Since his half-sister, Cheyenne was in town Christian decided to visit her at his dad's place. As afternoon turned to evening, Cheyenne indicated that she was hungry and stated she was craving something to eat that would be fitting for a pregnant lady. Christian agreed he was hungry and said he would go with her. For some unknown reason, Dag begged off leaving the house for dinner.

Christian with Cheyenne drove his pick-up truck down the hill into Hollywood. He suggested going to Musso and Franks Restaurant to which Cheyenne had no objection since their dad often hung out there with other Hollywood stars. They had no trouble being escorted to a cozy table in the back which afforded them some degree of privacy from the common tourist. Drinks arrived immediately, long before the food. The alcohol continued to flow and Christian downed them upon arrival. Earlier in the day he had consumed a six pack of beer with friends.

Christian was a quiet drinker and didn't become more talkative as he became more intoxicated. He sat at the table letting Cheyenne do most of the talking. Curiously, Cheyenne started on a diatribe complaining about her fiancé, Dag. She told her half-brother how Dag had verbally abused her and had slapped her around on various occasions. She painted a picture that Dag was violent toward her without any justification.

After a pleasant congenial dinner, Christian and Cheyenne left the restaurant together. Christian decided to drive by his apartment where he lived with his girlfriend to pick up his .45 caliber handgun. Then they proceeded back up the hill as Christian tried to negotiate all the twists and turns of Mulholland Drive arriving at the celebrated turn in the road named 'Bad Boys Curve". This was named for all the bad boys living on Mulholland Drive especially **Marlon Brando** and **Jack Nicholson**.

At the end of the curve, they pulled into a driveway closed by a tall wrought iron gate with sharp spikes to keep intruders out. Christian punched in the private code and the gates swung open. After pulling in, the heavy metal gates closed which meant everyone inside would be safe from criminals on the outside who could harm the Brando family.

They drove up and parked the truck to the side of the house. Both entered the silent house. Cheyenne told Christian she was tired and she excused herself to go to bed. Then Christian proceeded to the den where Dag was staying. He could hear the faint sound of the TV. When Christian entered Dag was lying on the sofa dressed in black shorts and brown short sleeve shirt. Dag's eyes were transfixed on the television which was on. With his one hand Dag was trying to roll a cigarette while holding a tobacco botch. His other hand was on the TV remote control as though he was adjusting the TV.

Possibly he was using the remote control to turn down the sound since Christian seemed to want to speak to him. Christian, without any hesitation, said to Dag, "Are you slapping around my sister?" "Look it, don't do that anymore!" Christian quickly approached and surprised Dag who was still lying on the sofa. Christian moved forward with his hand holding the .45. What happened in the next nana-second has been widely debated. What is known for certain was that the .45 handgun was fired with a bullet entering the cheek of Dag and exiting from his neck. Was the shooting intentional or accidental? Was it premeditated murder or something less?

CHAPTER 22

SHOOTING IN MARLON'S HOUSE

Marlon's two-acre estate on Mulholland Drive consisted of three buildings divided into 12 rooms that Marlon described as a house with add-ons. Marlon cherished his privacy and always had his bedroom separate and apart so he wouldn't be disturbed by all his children running in and out of the house.

The sound of the .45 caliber handgun going off made a piercing sound that jarred everyone awake. Marlon jumped out of his bed and raced to the den where the sound appeared to originate from. Others came running out of their rooms to figure out what was that loud sound. When Marlon entered the den, he saw Christian standing over Dag lying on the sofa. Christian seemed to be mesmerized looking at Dag's lifeless body. Seeing Christian standing with a gun in his hand and noticing blood on Dag's face, Marlon was trying to assess the situation.

For whatever reason, Marlon went into the 'save the victim' mode. Sensing that Dag wasn't breathing, Marlon tried to perform mouth to mouth resuscitation. After several moments of frantic attempts to revive Dag, the sobering fact was it was too late to save Dag. Marlon's attention was directed at Christian who had a look on his face of 'I've got to get out of here before the cops get here.' Marlon recognized he was the only sober adult in the room and his immediate task was trying to keep Christian from running away. Christian was so drunk he didn't know how to react. His only comment to Marlon was, **"Dad I didn't mean to shoot him but he was coming at me."**

Marlon had his hands full dealing with a stoned distraught Christian so he asked someone else to call the police. Since the Brando estate is located on top of Mulholland Drive it took the LAPD considerable time for a police unit to reach the house. When the officers arrived, they were met at the door by Marlon. The officers could see Christian sitting on the floor trying to comfort Cheyenne who was distraught and incessantly crying. When the officers entered the den, they saw Dag's body lying on the sofa with his eyes wide open looking at the ceiling. They easily saw that the victim had a bullet hole in his face with a slight amount of blood oozing out of the neck area.

The officers examined the body and couldn't find any signs of life so they called for paramedics to respond to make a more accurate assessment of the victim's condition. The officers glanced down at the victim's hands and noticed one hand holding cigarette rolling paper and the other hand partially holding a TV remote control.

As the officers approached Christian, he said, "I shot him, man. But not on purpose. We were both in a fit of rage. The gun went off. Please believe me, man. I wouldn't do it in my father's house." Whether it was all the alcohol or the excitement of the moment, Christian couldn't stop talking. He went on to explain that Dag was shot as the two men struggled for possession of the gun.

The officers had heard enough and placed Christian in handcuffs. Since there was a dead body with a bullet hole through his head, the Hollywood detectives were called to come to the scene. The two night detective received the call to respond to Marlon Brando's house on Mulholland Drive. Within moments they left the Hollywood Station heading up to Mulholland Drive. No one knows for certain whether the night detectives were humming the tune 'Just think twice it's just another day in paradise' which was from a Phil Collins song which was a top album for 1990, '***Another Day In Paradise.***' The detectives had to wonder to themselves why so many people think of Hollywood as being Paradise.

CHAPTER 23

CHRISTIAN'S STATEMENTS

When the detectives arrived they conducted a homicide investigation which included a CSI team. The detectives wanted to determine where and how the victim was shot. They could see that the bullet entered the victim's cheek area and exited the back of the neck. The question was where was the slug that exited the victim's head? The CSI technicians examined the carpeting on the floor. A short distance from the sofa there appeared to be a slight hole in the carpet.

The technician poked a pencil into the hole and could feel something in the wooden floor. The pencil showed a .45 degree angle of the bullet entering the floor. The detectives looked at this angle and if that was true, then it proved that the victim was lying on the sofa when he was shot. In order to obtain a more accurate reading, the technician would have to remove the carpeting and padding to completely find the slug and obtain an accurate reading of the angle of the bullet.

The $64,000 question was, what LAPD detective was going give the order to cut up and make a giant hole in the carpet of Marlon Brando's estate on Mulholland Drive. This was the home of the world legendary Hollywood actor who played the Godfather. The head detective could envision being called into the chief's office and readout for cutting up Mr. Brando's home carpet in the den.

It was after midnight, who do you call for permission? The detectives huddled together and everyone agreed that the slug needed to be retrieved from the wooden floor. One suggestion was to make a long slit which wouldn't be so noticeable. Another opinion was to cut a two foot square hole with a sharp knife in hopes the carpet could be re-taped down. The group of detectives weighed the pros and cons. Everyone felt the pressure of the situation and the need to wrap up the investigation before the sun came up in the morning. It was never clear who said, "Damn it, just cut the carpet, let's get on with it." The group all nodded in agreement and left as one of the technicians took out a box cutter. He pressed down on the blade and in less than a minute there was a giant hole in Marlon Brando's carpeted den.

One of Marlon's sons, Miko, was standing to the side and he seemed surprised by the big hole. But within minutes he became fascinated as the technician found the slug buried in the wooden floor. The CSI technician was able to carefully remove the slug for a ballistic expert to analyze it to see that it was fired by the .45 semi-automatic owned by Christian.

A piece of doling was placed in the hole in the plywood floor and the technician measured the angle of the dole. The trajectory path of the bullet showed that the victim had to be lying down when he was shot. This turned out to be one of the most incriminating pieces of evidence. Now it was clear Christian wasn't telling the truth when he claimed that Dag was standing up struggling with him when the gun went off. The detectives were relieved that cutting up Marlon's carpet proved to be necessary to retrieve vital evidence.

The other observation the detectives couldn't help but notice was the fact that there didn't seem to be any signs of struggle in the den. The table and chairs were in place and nothing seemed to be knocked over or in disarray. Christian claimed that there was a struggle over the gun when it accidentally went off. This story didn't add up when looking at the furniture in the den.

As detectives were finishing up examining the crime scene and interviewing witnesses, other detectives had escorted Christian while in custody to the Hollywood station. After the initial processing, they brought him into one of their interview rooms. The detectives indicated to Christian that they wanted to get his side of the story as to what happened. They wanted to put Christian at ease so he would continue to be talkative. Back in1990, the city police stations were trying to go 'No Smoking.' They noticed that Christian was a chain smoker and the last thing they wanted to do was for Christian to have a nicotine fit. So the detectives made no mention to Christian about the No Smoking policy. First, they advised him of his Miranda rights. "You have a right to remain silent; you have a right to an attorney; anything you say can be used against you." They asked if he understood and he said he did and he was willing to talk.

As Christian took out another cigarette and lit it up, he comfortably leaned back in the chair. He exhaled filling the small interrogation room with a thick cloud of smoke. He leaned on the table with his elbows and started trying to tell a story to be the most helpful to himself. However, the amount of alcohol he had consumed that night had not worn off. He had .19% blood alcohol level which was almost three times the limit for a DUI driver. His problem was keeping his stories straight. He told one inconsistent story after another. His initial statement was about him bringing his gun collection to his dad's place for safe keeping and he was trying to get the .45 automatic he kept under the cushions of the den sofa. Christian said:

"I'm going to tell you the truth, and it was an accident. We got in a struggle. Had my .45 underneath the, you know, where he was lying down."

"We got in a struggle and the gun went off in his face. I didn't want to hurt him. I didn't want to kill him."

"You know, we got in a struggle, I said, 'Let go.' And I'd been drinking, you know, I had about three gin and tonics. I didn't, I mean, go up to him and go BOOM! In my dad's house. If I was going to do that, I'd take him down the road and knock him off."

When Christian was asked about his relationship with his sister and Dag he said the following:

"Yeah, we went out to Musso and Frank's in Hollywood. Just the two of us. He stayed home. And we talked about, how's life?"

"I went in the other room and I went back. He's lying there on the couch. I said, 'Get your fucking ass off the goddamned couch. I want my' You know, I couldn't get at it. I'd wanted to pull it out, and I was going to put it in the old man's room, all right, with the rest of my – you know, my $2,000 shotguns and that stuff. We got in an argument and he grabbed the gun."

"I just said, "Get up, I want to take it in the other room." And we started struggling with the gun, and there was one in the chamber. It was cocked. There was a round in the chamber, and"

A short time later Christian's story changed slightly by saying:

"I said, 'Get the fuck off the couch.'" "No. I'm watching TV." So, you know, he got up...like, you know, he was sitting on the pillow. I'm, I'm shaking. You know, I'm just trying to tell you. So I grabbed it, we had words." "Oh, I said, you know, 'What the fuck are you doing around here?'" "I said, 'Why don't you go back to the ...coconuts where you belong.'" "You know, and fuck you this and fuck you that. And...I didn't and He grabbed me, my wrist, with the gun, and that's it". "Then he didn't have time to say anything. It just went off. I let go. I said, 'What are you doing? This is not, then BOOM."

The detectives continued to question Christian and re-question him and the story began to change. His new version had him picking up the gun at his girlfriend's apartment.

"Oh, yeah I went over there to get it because that's how I got it." The detective asked, "So the gun was at your girlfriend's house? You picked up the gun there? Christian responded. "Yeah."

"I did it because he hurt my sister."

"He was laying on the couch. He was fighting with my sister. I said, 'You leave my sister alone.' We were both in a rage. The fucking gun went off."

"Man, death is too good for the guy."

Christian seemingly was digging a deeper hole for himself by continuing to talk. The detectives didn't want to shut him up but let him weave his web of all the inconsistent statements.

CHAPTER 24

MARLON'S STATEMENTS

Eventually, it was decided to get a search warrant for Christian's apartment which he shared with his girlfriend. When they started looking for other weapons or ammunition it wasn't long before they uncovered a large stockpile of weapons in the apartment. Many of the weapons were illegal to possess and others weren't registered. After the detectives confiscated the weapons they did an inventory. Later, when murder charges were filed against him, they also added charges for possession of illegal firearms.

The detectives wanted to get statements from everyone who was at the house at the time of the shooting. Marlon said, "About 15 minutes after their return, he became aware that they were in the den, and he left his bedroom to see what was going on. I found Christian holding a large handgun, and he told me that he had just shot and killed Dag. I told Christian to unload the gun and to give it to me. Then Christian affected an empty casing from the semi-automatic which landed on the table next to the couch. Then he handed me the weapon. And I put the gun under the cushions of the sofa in the nearby computer room. Christian was highly agitated and said he hadn't intended to shoot Dag, but that Dag had grabbed for the gun, which went off."

"I went into the den and found Dag lying on the sofa and I felt for a pulse and immediately called 911. I attempted to give Dag CPR but realized that it was too late. The TV was still on and I took the remote control device out of the dead man's hand and shut it off." (Immediately after turning off the TV, he placed the remote back where he found it in Dag's hand).

"Christian was angry with Dag because Cheyenne had said that Dag had beaten her up." Marlon added that wasn't true and he found Dag to be extremely nice to his daughter. He described Dag as being polite, low-key, and a fine young man." Marlon went on to say that, "Cheyenne had often been irrational and had made untrue allegations against family members in order to stir up trouble." Then Marlon was asked about Christian and he said, "He had always been a fighter and had a bad temper that he exploded violently when angry. He had been overprotective to his baby sister."

When they talked to Marlon he parroted back what Christian told him seconds after the shooting. "I killed Dag. He's dead Pop. I didn't mean to do it. ***He went for the gun and it went off."*** This statement locked Christian into a position that wasn't supported by the facts.

The detectives tried to calm Cheyenne down enough so she could make statements to them. She could best be described as 'a basket case'. She said that

Marlon wasn't her father, and that was part of what she and Christian were talking about. However, neither Cheyenne nor Christian explained exactly what they were talking about during dinner. The purpose for Cheyenne visiting Los Angeles was that she could receive mental help because of her frail condition. Was it all the alcohol and drugs she had consumed over the years that had affected her brain to the point that she could slip from lucid to irrational within minutes? Or, was it the fact that she always considered herself to be a 'Special Person'. While growing up she was the apple of her father's eye and she could do no wrong.

The word 'Pampered' would not fully describe how much freedom of development she received growing up in Tahiti. She would tell her classmates that she was the prettiest girl in Tahiti as well as the smartest. While growing up, no one dared tell her "NO". She was treated more like a royal princess rather than an ordinary child. Her view of herself was devoid of reality. Her unusual mental condition may be due to a distorted view she had about herself and those around her. She was acting like one of the top movie stars of 1990 which was Julia Roberts in ***Pretty Woman***. Cheyenne truly thought of herself as the Prettiest Woman of Tahiti.

When the detectives interviewed Cheyenne they were totally unaware of her fragile mental condition. They had no context to consider her statements in. She told them, "...the gunshot was no accident. It was a murder..." She went on to claim that her father and Christian's girlfriend had played roles in Dag's death. The detectives couldn't believe the venom she was spewing out as to those who were near and dear to her.

These detectives stepped back and reflected on what she was saying. Here she was trying to implicate her father who had reached out to her to bring her to Los Angeles for psychiatric help. Further, it was Christian who was trying to protect her from physical abuse by his confrontation with Dag. Why would she attack those who were trying to help her?

The following graphic page gives a summary of the Christian Brando cases.

Graphics 2

SHOOTING IN MARLON BRANDO'S HOUSE

May 16,1990

- Christian & Cheyenne came back from dinner
- Dag was lying on sofa watching TV in den
- Cheyenne went to her bedroom
- Christian confronted Dag
- He accused him of abusing Cheyenne

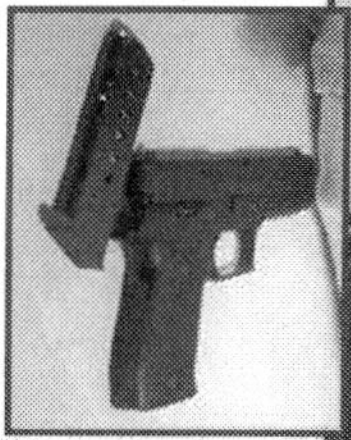

Christian's .45 Semi-auto

Item's in Dag's Hands

Christian Brando (32)

Cheyenne Brando (20)

Dag Drollet (26)

CHAPTER 25 WHO WAS MARLON BRANDO?

Almost every person in the Western world has heard of the actor, Marlon Brando. So, most people have formed an opinion about who he was partly due to the movies he appeared in as well as as what the magazines, books, and tabloids have written about him. Of all the information people have accumulated over the years, most people don't know some of the basic facts about him.

First off, he was born on November 3, 1924 in of all places, Omaha, Nebraska. He and Warren Buffett almost grew up together but both made a name for themselves in different fields. How could a Cornhusker from little Omaha become an actor? Well, it wasn't from his dad who was in the pesticide and chemical business. His mother did some acting in the local theater where she later volunteered her services. The ones who had the most impact on Marlon were his two sisters who enjoyed acting in various plays.

Early on, Marlon learned how to mimic any character he saw in the movies. He had an ear for hearing the inflection in voices and paid attention to the mannerisms of these actors. He could copy anyone. He was so confident in his talent that he came across as being somewhat cocky. He recognized he had some type of gift and he wanted to build on it. He moved to New York and he attended Stanislavski Acting School and learned the fundamentals of 'Method Acting'.

In 1947, he had an acting part in ***A Flag Is Born*** and some theater people noticed that he had some type of 'Raw Sexuality' which was appealing especially to young women. In that same year, he was casted in Tennessee Williams Broadway show ***Streetcar Named Desire.*** He was a big hit in his part and when they decided to make a movie of it, he was given the lead in the movie. This was a rare occasion since the wisdom at the time in Hollywood was to replace the Broadway stage actors with recognizable movie stars. The studio took a gamble in using him and it paid off big time for them and for Brando

Other movies followed such as ***The Men*** in 1950; ***Viva Zapata*** in 1952; ***Julius Caesar*** in 1953; and ***Wild One*** also in 1953. However, in 1954 it was the movie ***On the Waterfront*** with Eva Marie Saint that made him a truly big movie star when he won his first Academy Award for Best Actor. His career and his life changed at that point.

Later he did ***One-Eyed Jacks*** in 1961; ***The Chase*** in 1966; ***Reflections in a Golden Eye*** in 1967; and finally ***Burn*** in 1969. By this time in his career, his cockiness had earned him the reputation of being a 'difficult actor' which could cause delays and overruns for a studio. His career became stagnant and studios were avoiding him. It was not until 1972, when director Francis Ford Coppola asked Paramount Studios to permit him to use Marlon Brando as the Godfather. The Studio's answer was a firm "NO".

Paramount Studios had decided that they wanted Danny Thomas to play the Godfather role. Coppola refused to accept the idea of Danny Thomas as the Godfather and continued to demand Brando for the part. Not until Danny Thomas turned down the role did Paramount give the green light for Brando. In the end, Coppola was happy and the studio couldn't believe the money they made off that one movie. The big winner was Marlon Brando because he had become the real Don Corleone that movie lovers recognize all over the world.

This brought him another Oscar for Best Actor yet this time he was going to have some fun with the Academy Awards committee. He requested that a woman accept the award for him. What he arranged was having an Indian maiden by the name of Sacheen Littlefeather receive his Oscar and then instead of thanking the Committee for the award she started lambasting it. She went on complaining for several minutes on live television criticizing how the studios depicted Indians in the movies.

The success of the ***Godfather*** allowed him to perform in ***Last Tango in Paris*** where he gave a great performance even though the critics criticized it for having explicit sex scenes. After this movie, Marlon seemed to go into self-hibernation. His acting career was taking a back seat to his over use of alcohol and drugs which was confining him to his home on Mulholland Drive.

In 1979, Francis Ford Coppola thought he could get Marlon Brando to pull himself together to film ***Apocalypse Now***. However, when filming began, Marlon was way overweight and they had to shoot the film using lighting and shadows to cover up Marlon's extreme obesity. Francis Ford Coppola was surprised when Marlon showed up on the set without ever reading the script. It became almost unbearable but Coppola saw to it that the movie was completed. After the completion of the movie, Marlon retired from movie making.

For almost a decade he disappeared from the silver screen until 1990 when he did a supporting role in ***A Dry White Season*** about racism in South Africa. In his later years his passion and energies were directed to ecology, aquaculture, and the politics of race relations.

CHAPTER 26

MARLON'S WIVES

There was another aspect of Marlon's life that was even more bizarre than his movie career and that was as to his many wives and children. He had 3 ½ wives (the ½ is his housekeeper who he lived with and had children with) and a total of 11 children. Most members of the public have given up trying to remember the order of the wives. Also, his children had difficulty keeping up with all the new brothers and sisters who were unexpectedly appearing at family events.

Anna Kashfi, was his first wife, and they were married from 1957 to 1959 and she is important in this story since she was the mother of **Christian**. Anna was exceedingly attractive with her dark skin and almond shaped eyes. Her father was Welsh who happened to be working in India when he met his wife. Anna was born in Calcutta and later moved to London where she was spotted by a talent scout when she was working in a boutique. The agent was impressed with her beauty and she was given several parts in two Indian movies in 1955. She did well enough to be sent to Hollywood to appear in several American movies. She appeared in the ***Cowboy***

with Glenn Ford and Jack Lemmon. Later she appeared in ***Battle Hymn*** staring Rock Hudson.

Anna's natural beauty was exceptional. She exhibited an exotic foreign appeal which attracted Marlon. He insisted on being introduced to her. She was flattered to have the eye of Mr. Brando and he found her fascinating. They dated and there was a magnetism created which pulled them even closer. Marlon was so impressed he gave her an engagement ring and at the same time she announced that she was pregnant. The studios didn't know how to handle the two events without damaging both their careers.

It was agreed by the studios that they would be married in a secret ceremony on October 11, 1957. However, Marlon found it hard to give up his womanizing and he wasn't overly thrilled about the commitment of marriage. Within five months, Christian Brando was born on Mother's Day, May 11, 1958. This should have been a big day for Marlon in that he had a son to carry on the Brando name. However, he didn't want to be tied down at this stage of his life. Marlon wanted out and the studios wanted the couple to wait for a convenient time when their movies wouldn't be harmed by the bad publicity which often occurs during a divorce.

By September 1959, Anna packed up her bags and picked up Christian who was about 16 months old and drove out of the Brando estate on Mulholland Drive for the last time. The studio approved the divorce and both went their separate ways. The only problem was that they had a son to raise between the two of them. The custody and well-being of Christian created endless verbal fighting to fill the next 18 years. Some reporters in the media claimed this was one of the most bitter child custody battles that Hollywood had ever seen.

Movita Castaneda, his second wife, from 1960 to 1962 and the least talked about wife in our story. She was born on a train in Mexico and became a well-known Mexican-American actress. She acted in numerous Western movies and her claim to fame was that she played a Tahitian girl in the ***Mutiny on the Bounty.*** This is where the public becomes thoroughly confused with Marlon's wives. What has to be remembered is that she appeared in the first ***Mutiny on the Bounty*** movie produced in **1935.**

Marlon was coming out of a bruising divorce in 1958 so he was looking for a woman who could provide some stability in his life. Movita had dark skin with almond eyes and a charisma that totally intrigued Marlon. Even though she was seven years older than Marlon, he found her irresistible and they were soon married. They had two children. Miko was born in 1960 and Rebecca was born in1966. Marlon and Movita gave the appearance of a typical Hollywood couple with a solid family life. Everything was great until the role of Christian Fletcher came along in a remake of the ***Mutiny on the Bounty*** and Marlon wanted to play that part. It was to be filmed in Tahiti near where the actual Mutiny on the Bounty occurred. In 1962, Marlon left home to appear in the making of the movie in Papeete, Tahiti.

Tarita Teriipia was his third wife and they were married from 1962-1972 and she became the most dominant of the wives because she is the mother of **Cheyenne.** How they met was a direct result of the movie he was acting in. A combination of bad weather and delays in the script required Marlon and the other film makers to spend months stranded in Tahiti. There wasn't much to do on the small island accept drink and womanize. It wasn't difficult to notice the native women of the island since the custom was for the women to be topless. The other custom was the fact that the women were extremely friendly and the men had no trouble of becoming intimate with them.

CHAPTER 27 MUTINY ON THE BOUNTY

As the weather improved, the producer realized that for the next day's shooting they needed to decide who was going to play the part of the Tahitian maiden who the character Fletcher Christian was scripted to fall in love with. The director was beside himself and asked Marlon where they were going to find an actress to play this part in the middle of the Pacific Ocean. Marlon said, "That won't be a problem." He assured them that he would find a Tahitian beauty to play the part.

The staff had assembled a large number of Tahitian young women to play the part of extras for the renowned scene in which Fletcher Christian and his crew arrive on the beach from their ship, the HMS Bounty. The young women were topless in minimum garb and Marlon went over to a group of them who had mixed French and Polynesian features. Marlon asked the dozen or so young women to stand up which they did in two separate rows. Marlon, with his critical eye for beauty, slowly walked between them. He gazed on each one from head to toe and he eyed their friendly warm faces. For any male this was like experiencing heaven on earth. All were truly gorgeous with their long raven black hair and 'come hither' smile and perfectly tanned body with young pointy breasts.

Marlon took his time in sizing them up and he tried to remember which ones he had been intimate with on the beach over the past three months. With all the alcohol he had consumed, he couldn't remember which ones he knew since to him they all looked alike. He realized he needed to find his co-star since they had to start shooting on the next day. The pressure was on and a decision had to be made.

Marlon stepped over to one of the beauties and asked her name. She graciously stepped forward and said in a soft French accented voice, "My name is Tarita Teriipia." Somehow her voice and her perfect Polynesian body somehow melted Marlon's heart. He then, matter of fact, said to her, "Come with me". He walked her into the bar used as the headquarters for the movie. He grabbed Tarita's hand and pulled her over to the director and he said, "Here is our new co-star for the part of Fletcher Christian's Tahitian maiden."

The director took one long look at her realizing the tight shooting schedule he was facing. Without any hesitation he replied, "OK, get her to sign a contract." Marlon took her over to the 'contract guy' to do the paperwork. The 'contract guy' asked her how much she wanted for her acting part. Tarita didn't know how to answer. Marlon tried to explain she would have to make herself available for the next several weeks. She explained that she worked in a hotel kitchen preparing meals for the hotel guests.

The clerk wanted a dollar amount to type in above the word 'compensation' on the contract. Then again he asked, "How much?" Again she didn't know how to answer. She recoiled back in embarrassment not knowing what to say. Marlon stepped into the conversation and asked her what she really wanted in the world.

Tarita waited a moment and an enormous smile came over her face. She spoke in a demure voice that was barely audible and said, "I would like a motor scooter." The clerk sneered not knowing how to type in 'motor scooter' for a dollar amount. Marlon said, "Is that all you want for being in the movie?" Tarita didn't want to be greedy in a mere whisper stated, "Maybe another motor scooter for my cousin."

The clerk quickly typed in that amount of compensation for Tarita's acting in the movie, ***Mutiny on the Bounty***, and was a total of 'two motor scooters.'

With the contractual issues resolved, Marlon then took his leading lady to his place to become acquainted. For the next several months Tarita was at Marlon's side on camera and off camera. It was impossible to know what Marlon fell in love with. Was it Tarita's beauty? Or was it the Tahitian way of life?

Even though Marlon was officially married to the actress, Movita Castaneda, who played the part of Fletcher Christian's Tahitian maiden in the movie in **1935**, he now had fallen in love with the new woman who was playing the Tahitian maiden in the new movie in **1962**. As confusing as this may seem, it was time to have the marriage to Movita annulled so he could marry his new Tahitian love- Tarita.

Marlon and Tarita were married in 1962 and they had two children, Teihotu and Cheyenne. Marlon loved his new life and in 1966 he bought an atoll where they built a home. They continued to enjoy life there. In order to make money Marlon was having to return to the States to make movies such as ***The Chase*** in 1966, ***Reflections in a Golden Eye*** in 1967, and ***Burn*** in 1969. It wasn't until Marlon got involved in the ***Godfather*** in 1972 that the marriage to Tarita was dissolved and he spent his time living in Hollywood in his Mulholland estate.

Maria was Marlon's housekeeper from Costa Rica who did a lot more than clean the house. Nowadays, we would most likely call her a 'significant other' even though Marlon was not formally married to her, but she basically took care of him for the rest of his life. She provided Marlon with three children: Ninna in 1989; Myles in 1992; and finally the last child, Timothy in 1994.

The bottom line was that Marlon had 8 children from his wives and housekeeper. However, over the years he adopted three additional children including Petra Brando-Corval, born in 1972; Maimiti Brando, born in 1977; and Raiatua Brando, born in 1982. When all the children are added up the total comes to **ELEVEN.** Needless to say 'Father's Day was a busy day for Marlon

CHAPTER 28

CHRISTIAN'S LIFE

Christian's life was as unstable as it could be with his mother and father constantly fighting for custody of him. But neither was capable of being a good parent. His father, Marlon, was too busy making movies and womanizing to have time to try to play the role as father. Christian's mother, who had an early career in movies, fell into a downward spiral of depression fueled by alcohol and drugs. Mentally and emotionally she couldn't perform as a mother.

The Marlon and Anna custody hearings were like a marathon soap opera. She accused him of beating her and he claimed that she had broken into his house. The issue of custody bounced back and forth like a Ping-Pong ball. In December 1964, Marlon was awarded custody because of Anna's perilous alcohol-drug problem. Then in 1965, a judge gave custody to Marlon's sister who took Christian to raise him on a farm in Illinois. However, he turned out to be a very wild uncontrollable child who didn't recognize any boundaries.

Eventually, Christian was returned to California and Anna obtained custody. That lasted for a short time until a judge in 1971granted joint custody requiring Christian to be enrolled in one of the many Ojai boarding schools in California. During the 60's and 70's, Ojai Valley, which was 80 miles north of Los Angeles, was the dumping ground for incorrigible children of busy movie stars. Ojai was the perfect place to warehouse difficult kids and keep them out of the bright lights of Hollywood.

By 1972, Marlon was consumed with the filming of the ***Godfather*** and ***Last Tango In Paris*** and didn't have time for Christian. This was a time when Anna was struggling with hopeless depression. Since Anna didn't have custody of Christian, she had him kidnapped and taken to Baja California where he lived a hippie life style. This came at a bad time for Marlon so he hired a private investigator to track Christian down and the PI was able to talk the Mexican authorities in allowing him to bring Christian back to the States.

Marlon was totally frustrated as to what to do for Christian. He remembered how much he had liked the Tahitian life style so he thought it would be beneficial to send Christian to his atoll in Tahiti. The hope was that he would assimilate with the other Brando children being raised by Tarita. However, as much as a good idea this was it didn't work out well so Christian was shipped back to the States. There, he was immediately enrolled in Cal Preps School in Encino, where he got involved with the 'bad boys' in the school and he excelled in drinking and pot smoking.

While attending the school in Encino, he lived with his dad in his Mulholland Drive estate as he continually got into trouble. In order to acquire the finest booze for his derelict friends as well as himself, he continually broke into their neighbor's house. That was none other than Jack Nicholson. One day when Christian was stealing several big bottles of Jack's first-class liquor, Jack came home and caught Christian in the act. Jack was furious and threatened evil things would happen to him if he ever did it again. Jack must have done a convincing acting job because Christian never stole from Nicholson again.

In 1976, when Christian was 18, he continued to receive poor grades and quit school. Marlon, as a father, couldn't understand how he continually gave Christian everything but he couldn't gain Christian's cooperation to merely going to school. At this point the best thing Marlon could do was let Christian try to survive on his own. So he kicked him out of the house and told him he was 18 and he was on his own.

From that point on, Christian found marginal jobs such as tree trimming and eventually welding to provide him a subsistence. However, his life seemed to come together as he reconnected with Mary M who he had known since they were twelve. When they were growing up they were considered part of the so called 'Mulholland Brats'. On January 28, 1981 Christina and Mary M married and Marlon permitted them to move in and live with him. She had a job working in a cosmetic store and Marlon gave her money to start her own store. She had more ambition than Christian who spent most of his time drinking, doing drugs, and womanizing. These were the traits he had learned from his dad.

During this period, Christian was flirting with danger by trying to hit on his father's starlet girlfriend, Jill Banner. She had appeared in several movies in the 60's and was working closely with Marlon on some new scripts. How could father and son womanize on the same 35 year old woman without sparks flying? Possibly her untimely death in1982 from an auto accident may have prevented father and son from coming to blows over the same woman.

Even though Christian was still married to Mary, they were having their differences. Christian's extreme violent temper was scaring Mary as he continued to threaten to kill her and her mother. By 1985, she had had enough and started divorce proceedings hiring the famous divorce attorney, Mervin Mickelson.

During this period Christian started associating with a rough crowd and he lived in a small dwelling on Laurel Canyon. He used the money he earned to purchase guns. He claimed he needed the weapons for protection since he was living in an isolated area of Laurel Canyon where dopers could easily rip him off.

At that time, Christian was making his living trimming trees. However, one day he took a bad fall injuring his leg. This was the time he met Laurene L, a blonde actress who sometimes worked as a go-go dancer and eventually found parts in various movies. She was ambitious and wanted to impress Christian so she bought him a $1600 chainsaw which definitely impressed him. As a result they became a couple.

By 1987, Christian's wife, Mary, wanted to finalize the divorce which resulted in her receiving alimony of $400 a month for six months. Although if she had waited she could have received a better settlement, but the threats from Christian were scaring Mary and her mother to the point they were fearful for their lives. She was willing to agree to any settlement as long as she could be rid of Christian and all his problems.

In 1988, Christian turned 30 years old. For most people, that is a psychological downer since it seems the fun part of life and carefree days are over. However, for Christian it was like having won the biggest lotto ticket of all times. Now he was of age to collect on the annuity his dad had set up for him years earlier. This meant he would be given $100,000 to spend every year for the rest of his life. This was on top of the $200,000 Marlon had spent to purchase a house for Christian located on Wonderland Drive which was located a short distance below Brando's estate on Mulholland Drive. With all this money at Christian's disposal, many parasites began to swarm around Christian in order to sponge off of his good fortune.

At this time Christian's life was starting to flourish. He automatically gained junior celebrity status as many children of Hollywood stars enjoy. The name recognition opens so many doors; however, the masses never receive the opportunity to pass through. This was useful for Christian in starting an acting career. He received various breaks possibly due to the fact that the producers wanted to curry favor with the celebrity parent or just assume that if the father had the skills to make it so does the son.

His name got him a part in the 1968 movie "The Secret Life of an American Wife." The movie starred Walter Matthau, Anne Jackson, and Patrick O'Neal and was considered a box office failure in making only $3 million. Although Christian had a minor part it was something to build on. Also, in 1968, he was given a role in "I Love You Alice B. Toklas" which starred Peter Sellers, Jo Van Fleet, and Leigh Taylor-Young. The film was about a character played by Sellers who fell in love with an endearing hippy who was noted for baking pot brownies. That movie wasn't a big hit or better described as a flop that went directly to rentals.

After two less than successful film adventures, Christian wanted to continue trying his hand at acting. An opportunity came along to do some acting in Italy. He went over and appeared in a movie, *The Issue at Stake* by Carmine De Benedittis, a TV executive. This movie didn't turn any heads and Christian came back to Hollywood looking for some other movie to work on. He got to know Bill C and they became close friends. Bill had a script titled *Brothers* which he was convinced would be a hit and he talked Christian into helping him out. Christian thought this could be the break he needed to follow his dad into show business. He and Bill tried to find someone who could pitch the script to the studio executives.

Christian couldn't get anyone to listen so he contacted his dad and asked him to make some contacts regarding the project. Marlon's response was, "I did things my way and you do things your way, good luck". Marlon may not have known how much Christian needed his dad's help. Without Marlon's help the ***Brothers*** project went into the trash can and Christian ended up returning to Laurel Canyon. Christian had the opportunity to appear in several movies but he didn't demonstrate any talent and he didn't create any magic on the silver screen. Because of his dependency on alcohol and drugs, he didn't have the drive needed to succeed even if he had a pedigree as the son of one of the greatest actors. Because of his built-in demons, he continually fell back on his skills of welding and tree trimming which were less stressful for him.

After Christian's failure to elicit his dads help on the *Brothers* project, his new friend Bill C, felt more than disappointed and decided to leave his wife and start all over in Hawaii. Christian thought if Bill didn't want his wife that he would have her move in with him. It was a gutty move but for Christian, then again, she appeared to be worth it. Many other men would agree when she became the Penthouse centerfold in 1989. However, when his friend Bill came back from Hawaii, Christian recognized maybe he had made a mistake on hitting on his wife.

Christian was contacted by his mother, Anna Kashfi, who had fallen on hard times after her second husband passed away. She begged to come to live with Christian since she had no place to stay. Christian felt sorry for his mother and bought a new bed so she could stay with him at his Wonderland house. When

Marlon heard about her staying at the Wonderland house, which Marlon had paid for, he issued an ultimatum to Christian, "Get her out of the house and get her a shopping cart. She's nothing more than a street person."

Christian was upset with his father and he and his mother moved out of the Wonderland house. He moved into a cheap apartment. He tried to rent the Wonderland house out to raise money so he could start paying his father back. There were strained relations between Christian and his dad.

Christian attempted to revive his acting career. He went to auditions and readings but he didn't have his heart in it and it showed. His life was spent scoring dope and trying to impress women wherever he could. The afternoons were reserved for zoning out by watching MTV.

He was struggling to find his own identity while enjoying his father's fame and support. He did coke (cocaine) to bring him up and used the beer to bring him down. He functioned as a tree trimmer with a bad leg and welder of art projects. He seemed to be a man who liked to work with his hands and didn't seem to adapt to the superficial world of Hollywood. Booze, drugs, and women were what motivated and his main hobby was collecting an endless supply of guns. That combination could ultimately prove to be deadly for him.

CHAPTER 29

CHEYENNE'S & DAG'S LIFE

Cheyenne Brando

Cheyenne was born in Tahiti into a loving family consisting of a father, Marlon, who was 46 and a mother, Tarita, who was merely 26. They lived in Tahiti like a king and queen with Cheyenne being their little princess. Understandably, Cheyenne thought well of herself and could be best described as an extroverted egotist.

She grew up as an outdoors girl who loved to surf, dance, and horseback ride. There was no question she was beautiful by any standard whether she was topless or not. And that may have been why Vogue wanted to use her in photo shoots. The name 'Brando' got her whatever her heart desired.

However, there was another side to Cheyenne in which she was like a fragile flower. At times she became deeply depressed and turned to alcohol and drugs to give her the nerve to make it through the day. When she didn't get her way she became uncontrollable.

By 1972, Marlon had moved on with his life by returning to the mainland. This was hard for Cheyenne to adjust to the fact that her father was gone. She thought she was the apple of her father's eye. She continually wanted to spend more time with him. Once or twice a year he came to Tahiti to visit his family but Cheyenne wanted a much closer bond.

When she was 19 she was insistent on visiting her father. He was starring in a movie in Toronto titled the ***Freshman***. However, Marlon had a hard and fast rule that he didn't want any of his children on any of the movie sets when he was filming. The purpose of the rule was that he didn't want them to see how he womanized and misbehaved.

When Cheyenne called him and asked if she could join him in Toronto, he immediately said, "No". Cheyenne wasn't in any mood to except a "No" for an answer. Her reaction was to go outside and find a car and drive as fast as she could down the narrow country roads. It wasn't long before she came to a curve and she lost control of the car. The jeep Cherokee she was driving hurled into the air and rolled over several times.

The first person on the scene after the accident thought Cheyenne was dead since her head had gone through the windshield. When help arrived, they were able to resuscitate her and take her to the local hospital where she was treated and survived. However, that may not have been such good news.

As a result of the accident, her face was totally disfigured. She suffered a broken jaw and a severed off part of her ear. Minutes before the accident she was a beautiful model that the magazines couldn't get enough photos of and now there was no way of putting humpty dumpty back together again. Because of Marlon's position and money, the best plastic surgeons were consulted and long term reconstructive surgery was begun.

What resulted wasn't a pretty picture and every time Cheyenne looked into the mirror her depression deepened. Her boyfriend, Dag, stayed with her and he tried to help but she was so fragile nothing seemed to comfort her. Then she learned she was pregnant and that sent mixed messages. The last thing she wanted was to be expecting a child.

Tarita related to Marlon the seriousness of the situation. Tahiti didn't have the mental health facilities that Cheyenne needed. Marlon decided to have Cheyenne fly to Los Angeles with her mother and Dag. There he would hire the best psychiatrist to help her through the depths of her depression.

In May of 1990, Cheyenne, her mother Tarita, and Dag Drollet came to Los Angeles and stayed at Marlon's estate on Mulholland Drive. To illustrate the concern that Marlon had, he ordered that all kitchen knives be locked up every night so Cheyenne couldn't harm herself.

Dag Drollet

Dag was from a prominent family in Tahiti. He met Cheyenne in a very unusual way. He was working as a construction worker and was in charge of supervising the building of bulkheads and the piers on Brando's atoll. He was a handsome guy, tall, and weighing 225 pounds. He was physically fit and liked the outdoors and he enjoyed racing motorcycles as a hobby.

Although he was six years older that Cheyenne they had a lot in common and were together for three years going from dating to living together. He really cared for her and realized after the accident that she needed some professional help with her severe depression. He was pleased when Marlon offered to have her come to Los Angeles for help. He wanted to be with her to encourage her with her therapy.

CHAPTER 30 BAIL HEARING

The first appearance in court was a big moment for Christian and the Brando family. Marlon was in the front row of Division 91 of Los Angeles Municipal Court and holding the hand of Tarita his third wife. He was surrounded by many of his children. They were there to show their unconditional support for Christian.

During the early hours of the morning, after the shooting, Marlon called William Kunstler who was the most recognized attorney in America at that time. He had gained fame in his civil rights cases that were highly publicized. The first phone call made by Marlon woke up Kunstler, and he said, "The messenger of misery has visited our house." Kunstler had to wonder whether the person on the other end of the line was a crank caller or was someone highly intoxicated.

Once Kunstler was convinced it was truly Marlon Brando, he agreed that he would represent Christian and come to California when he was needed. Six days after the shooting, there was the legendary William Kunstler appearing in the court and was seated next to Christian Brando. Marlon had to be proud of himself getting the most prestigious attorney to represent his son. If his objective was to intimidate the DA's Office, his plan fell considerably short.

As Christian sat in his orange jail jumpsuit, his attorney rose to address the court as to the bail hearing. Kunstler with his tall lanky frame made an imposing presence. His rugged, wrinkled face made for a scary appearance. However, his booming voice could be heard in every corner of the courtroom. He said, "This is going to come down to a tragic accident. A confrontation over an alleged attack on Mr. Brando's daughter, Cheyenne, by the deceased, and a confrontation and accidental discharge of a firearm."

Kunstler continued by explaining that Christian and Mr. Brando had turned over to the police all the weapons they both had possessed. With great pride Kunstler stated that Christian made no attempt to flee the crime scene, his father had called 911, he remained at the house, and in addition, he has cooperated with the police 100 percent.

Then to add the sure thing he said that Christian couldn't flee to Tahiti since he wouldn't be welcome there because of the Drollet family being so prominent there. He further pointed out that Christian was an ordinary young man of modest means who only had $100,000 from his trust fund to live off of. He earned his living by doing ordinary jobs as a tree trimmer and as a wielder and rented a place from his father.

Everyone in the courtroom could recognize, on their own, that the Judge, Rosemary Shumsky, was a middle-class black. Kunstler closed by bringing up the civil-rights movement by saying "I knew Christian when he was fourteen years of age, when I first met his father in the civil-rights movement, and I have been a friend of his father in that civil-rights movement since 1972." Kunstler continued to insert the words 'civil-rights movement' into his argument for setting bail in this Bail Hearing.

Kunstler turned the proceedings over to one of his assistant attorneys who discussed how famous people are often dealt with more harshly than regular people. This was the opposite argument that Kunstler's group generally claimed. The assistant finished by saying, "I would ask your honor to treat the defendant as if he were any other defendant without the Brando name."

With the Defense finishing, the prosecutor, Steve Barshop, rose up from his chair. The media had labeled him the 'Jewish Cowboy from Texas'. A better description would be the double for Walter Matthau as one of the Grumpy Old Men. He didn't mince words and directly addressed the court by saying, "This is a no-bail case!" He backed it up by citing the seriousness of the offense as well as the Superior Court Felony Bail Schedule.

The prosecutor then started reciting the facts of the case which the Defense had skipped over. He explained that the defendant had gone to his girlfriend's house to get the murder weapon on the way back from dinner, enroute to his father's house. The wound to Drollet's left check was a contact wound at an angle of .45 degrees, indication that the victim was shot while seated. The deceased, after death, was still holding a Bic lighter, cigarette paper, and small pouch of tobacco in one hand and a TV remote control in the other, negating any theory of a struggle.

He finished by saying, "This case, for the purposes of this bail motion and at the present time, is a first-degree murder."

After the prosecutor's hard hits, Kunstler got back up and addressed the court by citing that Christian was intoxicated and concluded by saying, "I became involved in this case at the request of an old friend and companion along the civil-rights route.

But I know this family, I've had long experience with Marlon Brando, and it is an honorable family who has contributed a great deal to the country in many, many aspects other than just Mr. Brando's acting career."

At that point Kunstler felt he had painted a picture that a black female judge would sympathize with. Then Judge Shumsky, after listening for 40 minutes, thanked both sides and matter of factually without explanation stated, "The court finds no basis for setting bail in this case."

After the hearing, Kunstler, at a press conference, criticized the judge by saying, "That woman, without a moment's hesitation, said no bail after hearing what I call one of the best bail presentations. I don't know what pressures were applied on the outside. I just think that this was an outrageous decision and that she misused her power."

It was not long before everyone recognized that William Kunstler might be a famous civil-rights attorney but he was way over his head in a California criminal courts where he didn't know the law or wasn't familiar with the various legal procedures. Kunstler being no dummy advised Marlon to bring attorney Robert Shapiro into the case since Shapiro knew how to handle cases in the local courts.

CHAPTER 31 CHEYENNE IS KEY WITNESS

The prosecution was pleased that they had what looked like a slam dunk case. The prosecutor assigned to the case was Steve Barshop who felt comfortable having Cheyenne as a witness who could provide incite as to the dynamics of all the people in the house at the time of the shooting. The prosecutor recognized that Cheyenne was the crucial witness in the case.

Cheyenne had given the detectives a complete interview stating, "Christian had retrieved his pistol as well as a knife on the way back to my dad's house after dinner. He repeatedly said on the drive to the house that he would "bust on" Dag and that he shot Dag within minutes of parking the truck and following her into the den. Christian just walked in and killed Dag. The shooting was not an accident."

The DA's Office knew that Cheyenne was pregnant and planned to have the baby in America. The only issue was to make sure she would be able to come to court either before or after the birth of the child.

The DA's Office had received the assurance from Marlon that he would make Cheyenne available to come to court when she was needed. Some believed she was in the USA so the baby would be an automatic American citizen if the baby was born here. The DA's Office wouldn't bother her as long as she stayed at Marlon's house. In mid-June the prosecutor asked the Defense attorneys to make her available for some questioning. Then abruptly she was gone, on a night flight back to Tahiti.

The DA's Office immediately contacted the authorities in Tahiti and verified that she had returned to Tahiti in order to give birth there. The child had to be immediately placed in postnatal detox because of all the drugs Cheyenne had been taking. The question became how and when to have her return to L.A. for the trial. The DA's Office sent a foreign subpoena to Tahiti to be served on her. What was a shock to the DA's Office was that the Tahitian judicial system would not cooperate. They claimed that they were conducting their own investigation of the death of Dag Drollet since he was a national of Tahiti. As a matter of fact, Cheyenne was arrested in Tahiti for the crime of Accessory to Murder. The Tahitian courts wouldn't permit Cheyenne to leave until they had concluded their investigation.

As the time for trial approached the pressure was increased to have Cheyenne served with papers to return to the USA. However, Cheyenne overdosed on drugs and she went into a coma. After she came out of the coma, she attempted to commit suicide. The DA's Office went into court to demand that the authorities respond to the request to have her returned under the Reciprocal Witness Act to testify in the trial of her half-brother, Christian. The matter went up to their appellate court which ruled that she was mentally disabled. Their conclusion was that her returning to the States would damage her already vulnerable psyche. Even in the Los Angeles courts, a judge ordered the DA's Office to stop pursuing Cheyenne to get her to return to testify.

The bottom line was that Cheyenne wasn't going to return to testify against Christian. The DA's Office never had anticipated that they would not be able to obtain Cheyenne back for trial. As the realization set in, the prosecutor changed their strategy as to how to try the case against Christian. They thought they had the upper hand since they still had the highly incriminating inconsistent statements Christian had made to the detectives at the Hollywood LAPD station, during the early morning hours of the shooting.

CHAPTER 32

ADMISSIBILITY OF CHRISTIAN'S STATEMENTS

Christian had made numerous statements to the detectives. Some of those statements included the following: "The gun was under the sofa and it was an accident; I picked up the gun after dinner; and I just wanted to scare him." All the different statements showed he was trying to cover up what really happened.

The Defense filed a motion that these statements were obtained in violation of Christian's Miranda rights. The matter was set for a hearing in front of another judge. The judge selected for that task was Judge Larry Fidler, who was thought by both sides to be a fair and just judge. The detective who advised Christian of his Miranda rights took the stand and testified that he read from his Miranda Rights card which he used in all cases. He took his Miranda Rights card out and read exactly what he had read to Christian before the interrogation.

1. YOU HAVE THE RIGHT TO REMAIN SILENT.

2. ANYTHING YOU SAY CAN AND WILL BE USED AGAINST YOU IN A COURT OF LAW.

3. YOU HAVE THE RIGHT TO TALK TO A LAWYER AND HAVE HIM PRESENT WITH YOU WHILE YOU ARE BEING QUESTIONED.

When it came to the fourth part of the Miranda Rights, the detective stated he didn't read it to Christian Brando since he didn't think it was necessary to state:

4. IF YOU CANNOT AFFORD TO HIRE A LAWYER, ONE WILL BE APPOINTED TO REPRESENT YOU BEFORE ANY QUESTIONING, IF YOU WISH.

The detective stated that Christian was the son of Marlon Brando who was a famous and rich actor. He didn't think it was necessary to read and explain that specific Right which pertained to people who didn't have money to hire a lawyer. The Defense attorney began his cross-examination and asked how he arrived at the point that Christian Brando didn't need to know about having a free lawyer. Did the detective know the financial situation of Christian? Did he know whether Marlon had set up a trust to support Christian? Did he know for certain whether Marlon Brando was having financial problems?

The detective was trying to insert common sense into the giving of the Miranda Rights. This was a big mistake since the case law had made the Miranda Rights a rigid set of rules that must be adhered to the letter of the law. Judge Fidler didn't have any difficulty to declare that all of Christian's statements made to the detectives at the police station were **inadmissible** meaning the jury would never hear how Christian continually kept changing his story as to how the shooting took place.

That wasn't all the bad news for the prosecution. Christian's new attorney was able to talk the judge into setting bail at $10 million. Even as well off as Marlon was he couldn't come up with that amount. After the prosecution's case became substantially weaker, the Defense went back into court for another bail motion. This time the Defense was able to persuade a judge to reduce the bail to $2 million. Part of the agreement was that Marlon would turn Christian's passport over to the court. For most defendants this would still be prohibitive bail but not for Marlon Brando. He immediately put up his near and dear Mulholland estate as the security for Christian's release.

At that point Christian was elated and Marlon felt he was in control of the situation. This was a great day for the Brando Family as Marlon marched Christian out of the County Jail. They were met by a wall of reporters asking questions about the case. The reclusive Marlon Brando started talking to the news media and went on and on about how his son Christian was being persecuted by the prosecution.

CHAPTER 33

DISCUSSING A PLEA BARGAIN

When the prosecution lost the hearing on Christian's inconsistent statements, it seemed like a double whammy to the prosecution. It was like knocking the legs out from under the DA's case. The best evidence the prosecution still had left was the statement that Christian made to his father which was, "I killed Dag. He's dead, Pop. I didn't mean to do it. He went for the gun and it went off." But could the prosecution rely on Marlon to testify to that statement in front of the jury? Just relying on Marlon to keep Cheyenne in the country for the trial didn't work out well for the prosecution. How could they be certain that Marlon might not change the wording of what Christian had told him?

The Defense would seem to have all the aces as the trial date approached. Still, the DA had two big aces which prevented the Defense declaring victory. The prosecution still had photos and officers who could testify that Dag was lying on the sofa with tobacco rolling paper and tobacco pouch in one hand and the TV remote control in the other. The other ace was the fact that the CSI team would say that Dag was shot lying down according to the trajectory of the slug dug out of the floor. Christian's story, however, that there was a struggle between the two of them was not supported by the forensic evidence.

What the public and the media didn't know was that both sides had major problems with their side of the case. Maybe the prosecution would have enough to prove a Voluntary Manslaughter but proving Malice for Murder was going to be next to impossible to convince 12 jurors. A plea bargain might be the best way to settle the case. The DA agreed that if Christian pled guilty to **Voluntary Manslaughter** it would dismiss the Murder charge. The issue of sentencing would be left open to be decided by the judge.

The Defense attorney at this stage was Robert Shapiro and he was a master of working out plea bargains. He had been involved in the court system for years and knew the judges well. Both Marlon and Christian didn't have problems with the plea bargain but their main concern was what the sentence should be. **Involuntary** Manslaughter often resulted in no jail time or credit for time served. However, **Voluntary Manslaughter** was considered more serious and generally resulted in at least a minimum time in state prison.

Bob Shapiro, without a doubt, felt that he had a chance to convince the judge to give Christian a minimum amount of time in county jail. It is unknown what was said between Shapiro and his client but on January 5, 1991, Christian agreed to plead guilty to **Voluntary Manslaughter with the sentence to be decided by the judge**.

The news media and many of the general public were disappointed there would be no trial. Many hoped the trial would reveal tidbits of gossip exposing Marlon Brando's cloistered life in his estate on top of Mulholland Drive. The tabloids and daytime soap operas were hoping to hear about Hollywood's most dysfunctional family with all of its dirty laundry being aired for the world to see and hear. Without a trial the public would be deprived of hundreds of articles and thousands of words that would never be printed about Tinsel town's macabre dark side.

CHAPTER 34

SENTENCING

Three days were set aside for the sentencing hearing. The first day involved psychiatrists from both sides testifying to Christian's mental issues. The Defense had experts who painted a picture of Christian suffering from chronic depression and some diminished capacity due to extensive drug use. The other side showed him as a troubled individual like many other defendants but not an excuse for his conduct. The battle of the experts filled up the entire first day.

On the second day all the players were in place to play their respective roles in what some called a sad 'Greek Tragedy'. The star should have been Christian but the media and public had their eyes glued on Marlon who sat with one of his other sons in the spectator section. He didn't project the image of the onetime leading man of

Hollywood. He reminded people of the pale Godfather who seemed somehow lost without his consigliore to whisper in his ear.

Robert Shapiro asked the court if Christian's father could address the court. In a packed courtroom the judge couldn't say "No". At that point the overweight Marlon shuffled up to the lectern. He glanced over to Christian and looked straight at the judge and started on a long rambling emotional plea for leniency for his son. He blamed Christian's mother, Anna Kashfi, for being a poor mother and it was her fault for his son's shortcomings.

Here was what many considered to be one of the greatest actors of all time and without a script he didn't know what to say. Then he seemed to touch on some circumspection of his own life. He exclaimed, "I led a wasted life by chasing a lot of women. I think that perhaps I failed as a father." No one in the courtroom was going to argue with him that he was a failure as a DAD. The spectators in the courtroom craned their heads in order to better hear Marlon's mumbling to the court. Everyone wondered what in the world was he trying to say. He seemed to have lost focus that this was a sentencing hearing for his son not an indictment on his parenting skills. When he ran out of words he put his head down and hobbled back to his seat.

Next the judge asked if the victim's relatives wished to make a statement. Mr. Drollet, Dag's father, took the spot that Marlon had relinquished. He explained the loss of Dag to the family and friends in Tahiti. He requested that the judge sentence Christian to the maximum.

The prosecutor then concentrated on the violent behavior Christian had exhibited toward his then wife, Mary M. In one of the documents that had been filed in their lengthy divorce proceedings, Mary had described how Christian had threatened her and her mother on several occasions. In one incident, he pulled a gun on them and said he would shoot them. Those documents were introduced as evidence in the sentencing hearing. At the end of the prosecution Argument, Steve Barshop said that the defendant deserved no less than 16 years in state prison.

The Probation Department is required by law to prepare a so called 'P and S Report' (Probation and Sentencing) that is presented to the judge to provide an objective opinion as to what the appropriate sentence should be. What was strange was the Probation recommendation was for only three years in State Prison. They were placing the emphasis on the fact that he didn't have any felony convictions and most of his problems related to his abuse in using alcohol and drugs. Neither the DA nor the Defense was pleased with the Probation recommendation.

Finally Christian addressed the court and he didn't know what to say. All he could think of saying was, "If I could change places with Dag, I would." Although he may have been sincere in making this statement, there was no way he could bring Dag back to life. Bob Shapiro tried to accent the positive which was Christian didn't have a criminal record. However, there was no way he could eliminate the negative which was that Dag was dead. Shapiro tried to say that this experience had been enough of a shock to straighten Christian out. No additional time in custody would have any impact on Christian.

Judge Thomas had to make a decision as to what the sentence should be. He had listened to all the speakers and could feel the intense interest in this case. If Christian didn't receive a significant sentence, it would appear that shooting an innocent person who was merely rolling a cigarette and watching TV was acceptable. The judge cleared his throat and with a firm voice stated that Christian Brando should serve 10 years in State Prison.

The question was who was more shocked to the 10 year sentence; Marlon, Christian, or Bob Shapiro? They had agreed to an 'Open Sentence' and may have been too optimistic as to the outcome. Granted, a jury could have convicted him of First Degree Murder which would have raised the sentenced to 25 years to life. Although at this stage, it was only a Voluntary Manslaughter which deserved less prison time than murder.

The sentence was imposed and the Department of Corrections decided to house Christian at San Luis Obispo Men's Colony which is located halfway between Los Angeles and San Francisco. Although, prison wasn't a pleasant place, the Colony was a productive prison since they had education programs for the inmates if they wanted to take advantage of them.

Fortunately for Christian, he received his high school diploma from the prison as well as worked in the machine shop to learn some skills. It turned out to be a positive experience for Christian but maybe not so for Marlon. Most weekends Marlon would find someone to drive him all the way to the prison in San Luis Obispo. The little city was better known for its old Mission and the main campus for California's renowned Cal Poly Engineering and Agriculture University.

The guards at the entrance to the Men's Colony were always unnerved when Marlon Brando, the Godfather, would arrive in his limo. It just seemed out of character for the Godfather to be visiting his son in a state prison.

Marlon became acquainted with every curve and hill in the long four hour drive up the old 101 highway and four hours back to his estate on Mulholland Drive. It is described as one of the nation's most scenic highways but for Marlon, the pleasant views of the Pacific Ocean only reminded him of the long, lost days he had savored on his atoll in Tahiti.

CHAPTER 35 LIFE GOES ON FOR THE BRANDO FAMILY

While Christian continued to check off the days in prison, his half-sister Cheyenne wasn't enjoying life much more than he was. Her return to Tahiti wasn't all that pleasurable. The Tahitian authorities charged her with Accessory to Murder for her involvement with Dag's death. Later, that charge was dismissed but it was like a dark cloud always floating over her head wherever she went on the small group of islands.

The Drollet family was well respected and wherever Cheyenne went she was reminded that she was the one who caused Dag's death. Even her best friends shunned her reducing her number of friends to a very small circle. Being a young mother with all the responsibilities that went along with having a baby was too overwhelming. She didn't know who to rely on. Because of the problems she had created in the States, she couldn't return to live with her father. Her mother was the only one still by her side.

Her depression swept her down a dark hole with no way out. She grabbed a hand full of sleeping pills which she felt would end all the misery. It almost worked but she was rescued at the last moment. Because of her instability, the custody of her son was taken away from her and given to Dag's parents. This should have been a wakeup call to her. Losing her son brought home to her the fact that she was a total failure in that she wasn't considered capable of taking care of her child.

Almost five years from the date of the shooting, Cheyenne was successful at what she wanted most and that was death so she could be with Dag. Her wish became a reality when she hanged herself in her mother's house. She may have been at peace but her dad had the difficult task of asking the Drollet family if Cheyenne could be buried next to Dag in the Drollet's family cemetery plot. As much as Mr. Drollet blamed the Brando family for the death of their only son, he was gracious enough to allow Cheyenne's casket to be placed next to Dag's.

Cheyenne was 25 years old when she ended her life which had been filled with so much unhappiness and full of tragedies. However, for Christian, his life mellowed out after his release from prison in 1996 after serving five years. He was placed on parole and moved to Kalama, Washington to try to restart his sad, unproductive, and squandered life.

CHAPTER 36 CHRISTIAN'S ENCOUNTER WITH BONNY

Christian's relocation in Washington State may have been the happiest days of his life since he didn't have to pretend to be somebody he wasn't. People in this rural community didn't have any preconceived ideas how Marlon Brando's son should act and behave. He fit in and the locals came to consider him just a 'Regular Guy'. As much as he thrived in Kalama, he still missed the Hollywood scene. He frequently came back to the Los Angeles area to visit friends and womanize.

Christian knew that Chadney's in Burbank was the place to meet 'friendly women'. This was a jazz band club that catered to the mature Celebrities who had reached their zenith. Their names were well-known but due to alcohol, drugs, or old age they weren't at the top of their game. Most of the old timers would roll in late in the evening to find a woman who wanted to provide an old Celebrity a 'Good Time'.

Regulars dropping by Chadney's were the likes of Dean Martin and Robert Blake who looked for any woman interested in spending some 'quality time' with an old Celebrity. For Blake it was the opportunity to escort the lovely lady to his travel van outfitted in the back with a timeworn used mattress. He always parked his so called 'Love Mobile' just out near the side door of Chadney's parking lot. This was so much more economical in that the old Celebrity didn't have to waste time or money on a motel room.

In early 1999, Christian made continual visits to Chadney's hoping his dad's name would transfer a little action his way. What amazed him was the endless supply of women who were looking for any type of Celebrity to spend time with. During this period he came into contact with Bonny Lee Bakley. She had her Lonely Hearts scam that provided her a decent living. She used soft porn photos of herself to mail to lonely men who would send her money.

When Bonny learned who Christian was she started zeroing in on him. She saw Christian as a good catch. As Bonny advanced in years she recognized that she would never make it as a Celebrity so for her, the next best thing was to marry a Celebrity. For Bonny, there was nothing more important in her life than being called a 'Celebrity Wife.' Even an over-the-hill star was good enough for Bonny. But in Christian's case she could easily get used to the sound of being addressed as 'Mrs. Bonny Brando'.

Still for Bonny it wasn't easy for her to close the deal by walking down the aisle. For these old timers, the last thing they wanted was another wife. Bonny had to find a way to force the Celebrity to marry her. Then it dawned on her, if she became pregnant the old star would have to marry her for the baby's sake.

Sometime around October of 1999, Bonny was running out of time so she had to step up the pace to make sure she would get pregnant. She started taking 'Fertility Pills' to speed up the process. Of course, Bonny told the men not to worry about her becoming pregnant since she was on the 'Pill' to which the men thought she meant the Birth Control Pill. If and when she became pregnant, the excuse would be that those darn pills didn't work. Of course, that was a little 'White Lie' since the 'Fertility Pills' did in fact work.

However, this was a time in her life when she couldn't rely on only one Celebrity so to maximize her effort she started sleeping with multiple sperm donors. She was concerned that some of the old timers might not have any silver bullets left in them.

She had been spending considerable time with Robert Blake in his 'Love Mobile' but when Christian was in town she would hook up with him since he was younger and more likely to be still fertile. However, Bonny became concerned about the relationship with Christian. She had heard that Christian hadn't been overly successful. She thought that he might not be able to support her the way she wanted, so she decided to turn her attention and affection to Robert Blake. She wrote a letter to Blake stating, "Hi, I hate to tell you this, but the pill didn't work for me." But Blake wanted her to have an abortion which Bonny didn't want to do. In reality, Bonny wasn't opposed to an abortion for religious reasons but because she had worked so hard to become pregnant.

When Blake didn't agree to marriage, Bonny's fall back plan was to work on Christian. When Bonny discovered she was pregnant she assumed the father was the youngest of her male companions, which was Christian. When the baby was born on

June 2, 2000, she named the child 'Christian Shannon Brando' and it was then time to step up the campaign to get Christian to the altar.

When it came time to do a DNA test on the baby, the big surprise was that Robert Blake was the undisputed father. Christian had to have been relieved and he decided to get out of town as quickly as possible. It seemed he made the right decision not to get too involved with 'Bad News Bonny'. Robert Blake became the target of Bonny's insistence on getting married. As much as Blake hated Bonny he definitely fell head over heels in love with the baby who was cute and cuddly.

Blake didn't want his lovely little daughter to be raised by a 'soft porn queen'. He begged Bonny to give up her mail order business which had supported her for years. She had worked so hard to develop the 'Lonely Hearts' scam that she didn't want to abandon it. Blake realized that he couldn't stop his daughter's mother from being in the' soft porn' business.

Blake couldn't figure out any alternative but to find someone to 'Whack Bonny'. He contacted his old buddies from the stunt department and asked them if they could get rid of Bonny. He couldn't convince anyone to help him so he told them if they would not help him he would have to do it himself. On January 17, 2005, after having dinner with Blake, magically Bonny was shot to death in Blake's car. Blake claimed he went back to the restaurant to retrieve his gun that he had left on the restaurant seat.

The DA's Office eventually filed murder charges against Robert Blake. During the trial the Defense representing Blake subpoenaed Christian Brando to testify to a statement he had made to Bonny which was, "You're lucky somebody ain't out there to put a bullet in your head." The Defense wanted to use this testimony to show that there were many old men who were out to get Bonny for defrauding them over the years. Christian wished he had never made the comment since he didn't want to cause problems for Bonny's family. Christian refused to testify in Blake's criminal trial.

The judge in the Blake murder trial ruled that Christian didn't have to testify in the criminal matter. Christian felt he had been lucky to dodge the bullet. However, his optimism didn't last long. Although Blake was able to obtain a not guilty verdict in his criminal case, Bonny's relatives didn't give up and filed a wrongful death civil suit against Blake.

When that civil case came up for trial, Blake's attorney subpoenaed Christian to testify for the Defense. Unfortunately for Christian, he found himself mixed up in someone else's business which he had no interest in. Trying to be the good guy Christian didn't want to testify to anything that would be harmful to Bonny's children. He, therefore, decided not to testify in the civil lawsuit against Blake.

However, the price was that Christian was found in contempt of the court for failure to testify and eventually had to pay a fine of $1000. The irony was that Blake got off on the criminal case and refused to pay anything on the civil suit. The only person who paid a price for the killing of Bonny was none other than Christian. He didn't have anything to do with her death but he was found in contempt and paid just because he was trying to be the 'nice guy' and not harm Bonny's family from winning a civil judgment against Blake.

CHAPTER 37

CHRISTIANS STRUGGLE TO FIND HAPPINESS

The entire Robert Blake and Bonny Bakley situation made Christian recoil back to Kalama, Washington to return to the simple life. However, it seemed that Christian had a target on his back seeking misery. Somehow between 2003 and 2004 he met Deborah Presley who claimed to be Elvis' illegitimate daughter. They seemed to have a lot in common since both were children of legendary fathers. It seemed like a natural union to have the son of the greatest actor marry the daughter of the greatest singer of all times.

They both had struggled in trying to find a happy personal life. Their marriage seemed to have so much in common. However, after a year of marriage there were signs that this marriage was not Camelot revisited. Christian's addiction to alcohol and drugs torpedoed the union and the spousal abuse brought the authorities into play and Christian was back in criminal court. He recognized he had a problem and plead No Contest to the charges and he was placed on probation with counseling for alcohol and drugs.

With all the counseling, the rocky marriage couldn't survive all the obstacles that confronted the two who should have had an ideal life hanging onto the coattails of their respective dads. A divorce was an unfortunate result which left both of them wondering if they were ever going to find happiness in life.

Christian retreated to his rural hideaway and was reluctant to get involved with other women. However, he met Mary Wilson (Pseudonym) and they started living together. This provided some stability in his fragile lifestyle. In the beginning of January 2009, he became ill and returned to Los Angeles for treatment. On the 26th the announcement was made that Christian Brando had died of pneumonia in a Hollywood hospital. This sent shock waves through the tabloids. How could Christian die at the early age of 49? Rumors started spreading that he had AIDS which weakened his immune system to the point his body couldn't continue to fight the AIDS virus. What the truth was most likely will never be known and really isn't important. Many reflect back on Christian's chaotic life and wonder did he ever have a chance for a good life. The minister at his funeral may have stated it correctly when he said, "He had a hard life, he really did. That's true of a lot of people who are born into fame."

However, controversy never seems to escape Christian. Even after his death his mother Anne Kashfi sued Christian's girlfriend for improperly spreading the contents of Marlon's ashes which had been given to Christian. After his father's death, certain members of the family were given separate urns containing Marlon's ashes. Christian was one of the recipients of one of the urns. Christian didn't know what to do with his father's ashes so he just kept them with his personal belongings. Christian, having died unexpectedly, meant it was up to his new girlfriend to tidy up Christian's personal matters. She didn't know what to do with Marlon's ashes but she remembered Christian mentioning that his dad liked to visit a certain park off of Laurel Canyon Drive.

The girlfriend thought she was doing the right thing in spreading Marlon's remains in the local park. Somehow the news media learned about this and when they contacted Anna Kashfi, she became enraged since she was designated to be the executor of Christian's estate. She was the one who should have received the urn containing Marlon's ashes.

What is strange was the fact forty years earlier Anna Kashfi, Marlon's first wife, had written a book about Marlon titled "Brando For Breakfast" which was less than flattering about Marlon. She would not appear to be one who would be in great reverence of Marlon's ashes.

After Anna Kashfi divorced from Marlon, her film career seemed to fizzle out. At the time of Christian's death, the news media announced that Anna was living in a trailer park in San Diego with her cat, with no real income except what she could earn from cleaning houses. The Brando curse had touched Christian's mother even though she hadn't been called "Mrs. Brando" for over 40 years.

The problems with all the urns containing Marlon's ashes was they were meant by Marlon to make amends for his lack of attention to his family members when they actually could have used his help. It may have been too little too late but it was a well-intended gesture by Marlon. Even Christian's last girlfriend had good intentions in sprinkling Marlon's ashes in a local park where children play. It will be interesting to see if any of the children who play in that park will someday become a great thespian from their contact with Marlon's ashes.

CHAPTER 38

MARLON'S LEGACY

Marlon really never got over Cheyenne's death in 1995. He withdrew into his master bedroom where he spent most of the remainder of his life. He had a housekeeper who took care of all his needs which included making babies. He truly became a recluse, distrustful of almost everybody. His only window to the outside world was by way of the telephone. He enjoyed talking for hours with old friends. What his phone companions didn't know was that he was recording many of these so called private phone calls. No one knew about the recordings except possibly the housekeeper. It was unknown why he wanted to record all these people. It might have been his intention to write a book about the glory years of Hollywood.

So much of his early acting years were focused on his image as the debonair leading man. However, in the latter years his appearance was the last thing he was concerned about. He became grossly obese which shocked anyone who he allowed to see him. From the year 2000 on, he let himself go and eating so much without any exercise was devastating to his health. Those close to him weren't surprised about his death on July 1, 2004, at the age of 80. He could best be described as a tired old man who had lived his life too quickly and may have spent too much time smelling the roses. Or, some might say picking the roses for his carnal pleasures.

He had one passion that he never wavered even at the end. He loved his atoll Tetiaroa which is 35 miles from the main Tahitian Island. Marlon always dreamed of developing the 12 islands that made up his atoll. There was no doubt that the atoll he purchased in 1966 had a gorgeous landscape with waving palm trees on pristine sandy beaches with the gentle roar of the surf. Could any person on earth not love this setting for a place to visit or even call home?

Over the 40 years Marlon owned Tetiaroa, he grew to understand there are issues when one mixes paradise with people. Years earlier he built on the atoll several bungalows for his family and invited guests could stay there. He even built in an airstrip to make it convenient to get to his atoll. He soon learned that in order to make the place livable one had to do things that were adverse to the pristine environment. All his adult life he tried to conceive of a way humans could enjoy an experience at his atoll but at the same time do as little damage to the environment.

Just before Marlon's death he had signed an agreement in which he sold part interest to developer Richard Bailey to create an eco-friendly luxury hotel on his atoll. This adventure has taken years and millions of dollars and finally in August 2014 the Brando Hotel had its grand opening. The initial visitors were highly impressed with the 35 luxurious hotel units with stunning views of the beaches. All the amenities of a five star hotel are met with outstanding world class restaurant. The private bungalows are merely $3,700 per night which may not make them available to all the natives.

Unfortunately, Marlon will not be present to see his dream come true. However, the visitors might be able to feel the presence of Marlon since some of his ashes were purposely spread throughout the atoll. For those who have a fondness for Marlon will enjoy their time visiting his paradise of Tetiaroa.

However, the Brando mystic still permeates Tahiti. In the main city of Papeete one can visit the cemetery where Cheyenne and Dag are buried together in the Drollet burial plot. It seems so surprising to see this truly Romeo and Juliet couple resting together after their tumultuous lives. What one thinks about is how magnanimous the Drollet family had to be to permit Cheyenne to be buried there after all the heartache she had brought to their family.

However, the union of Dag and Cheyenne still lives on in Tahiti in their son, Tuki Brando. Tuki was raised by the Drollet family and spends much of his time with his grandmother Tarita, Marlon's third wife and mother of Cheyenne. Tuki possesses the prominent features of the Brandos. As a result, he has done modeling for Versace menswear and appeared in numerous magazines. However, he wants to carve out his own life far from the entertainment world. He plans to go into the field of medicine when he finishes his higher education. What has perplexed many is why Marlon excluded him from his will. It would seem that Cheyenne was so intertwined with Marlon's later years that her only child had to be a major concern of his.

One of the most interesting characters of the Brando saga is Tarita, She still lives in her beloved Tahiti and is well respected by the natives. She definitely has lived the **Cinderella story** by working as a maid in a hotel kitchen and days later falling in love with the most handsome movie star of the time. Others would argue that she really lived the life of Guinevere from Camelot by living with prince charming for ten years in one of the most beautiful places on the earth called Tahiti. All have to admit that Tarita has lived one of the most fascinating lives that most women can only dream of.

SEX CRIME ON MULHOLLAND DRIVE

PEOPLE vs. ROMAN POLANSKI

CHAPTER 39 PHOTO SHOOT AT JACK'S PLACE

Next door to Marlon Brando's estate is Jack Nicholson's home. Both stars utilized the same driveway to enter their Mulholland Drive hilltop homes. Since both men were major womanizers, their driveway iron gates opened and closed for certain special starlets who made frequent visits. There wasn't anything surprising about attractive women coming and going from these hilltop bachelor pads. However, on March 10, 1977, there was a female visitor who forever changed this hillside retreat.

For Marlon Brando, 1977 found him between staring in the ***Last Tango in Paris*** and before he starting filming of ***Apocalypse Now.*** His career had reached its pinnacle and the offers were drying up. His stream of starlet visitors was dwindling as he spent most of his days eating himself into oblivion tucked away in his private bedroom.

However, Jack Nicholson's career was like a rising star in 1977 after finishing up the successful film ***One Flew Over the Cuckoo's Nest*** which permitted him to take on more unusual roles. Since Jack and Marlon were neighbors and both had been recent Oscar winners, Nicholson wanted to do a movie with his good neighbor. In 1976, the opportunity came along for both of them to star together in ***The Missouri Breaks.***

Although it wasn't the hit that critics had anticipated, it did allow the neighbors to play off of each other's characters.

Several years before, in 1974, Jack Nicholson had starred in ***Chinatown*** directed by Roman Polanski in which he and Nicholson became bonded in their friendship. Nicholson felt the pain that Polanski was going through after his wife Sharon Tate was brutally murdered by the Manson Family members on August 8, 1969. Because of Nicholson's busy schedule he was often away from his home when he had to be on a movie location.

Our story begins in 1977 on the date of **March** 10th. This was not a famous day in history except for those who are telephone enthusiasts. That was the day in 1876, when Alexander Graham Bell made the first successful telephone call by saying "Mr. Watson, come here, I want to see you." However, on March 10th in 1977, Roman Polanski made a call to his colleague Jack Nicholson to ask him if he could use his house for a Vogue Photo Shoot. Jack indicated he would not be around but Polanski could use his house. He explained that the maid would be around in the morning, but would be out of the way by the afternoon. Jack didn't know any details about the photo shoot and trusted that Roman would take care of his place.

The following graphic page summarizes the facts involving the Roman Polanski case.

Graphics 3

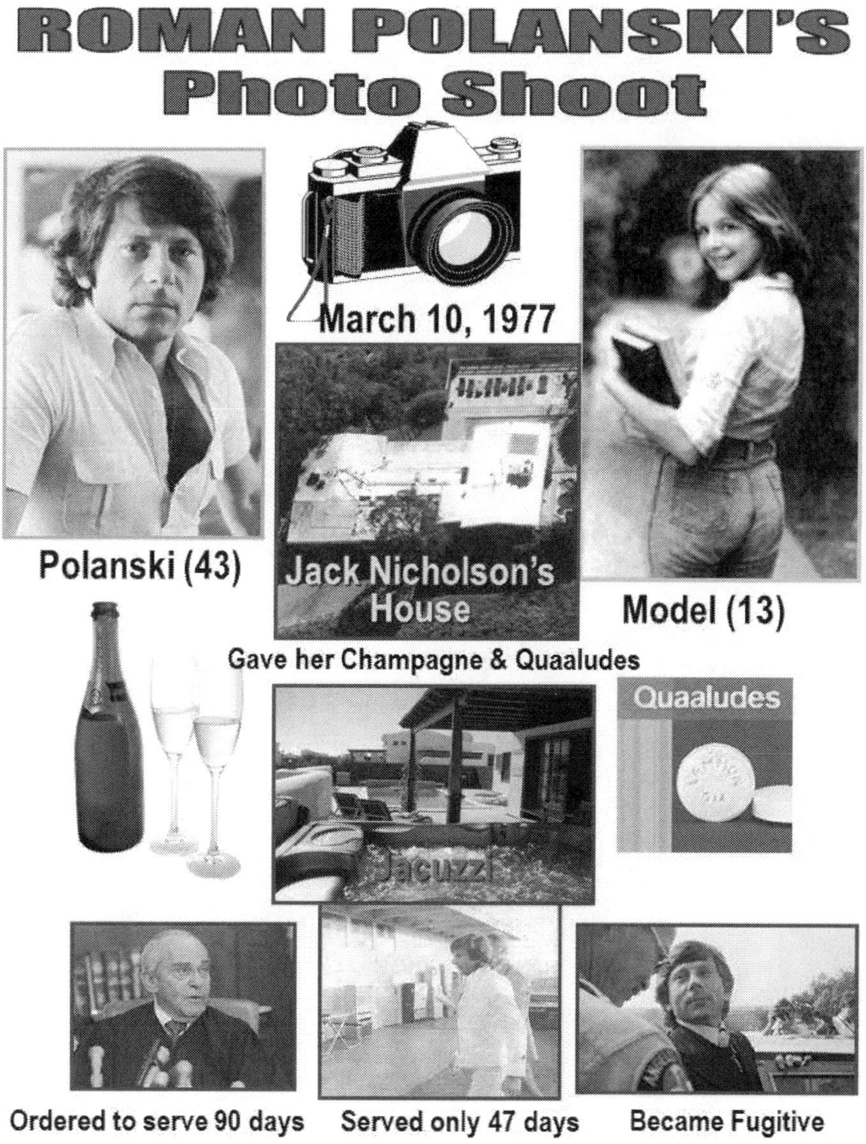
ROMAN POLANSKI'S
Photo Shoot
March 10, 1977
Polanski (43)
Jack Nicholson's
House
Model (13)
Gave her Champagne & Quaaludes
Quaaludes
Jacuzzi
Ordered to serve 90 days
Served only 47 days
Became Fugitive

Weeks earlier, Polanski had met Mrs. Gailey, a wannabe actress, at a social function. She had mentioned to him that her 13 year old daughter was doing some modeling and was hoping that she could be noticed in order to advance her career. During part of the conversation he made mention that he did photo shoots for European magazines and might have something coming up. Several weeks later, Polanski called Mrs. Gailey and explained that he was doing a photo shoot in the San Fernando Valley and asked if her daughter would be interested. Mrs. Gailey was surprised to hear from Mr. Polanski and assured him that she would have her daughter ready whenever he was doing the photo shoot.

The details were worked out and her daughter, Samantha, was excited to have the opportunity to go on a photo shoot with Mr. Polanski. He came by and picked her up and drove her to various locations. He had her pose for various photos and he was impressed by her innocent smile. Nothing seemed unusual about the event except at the end he told her that he wanted to take some photos for the European market. He asked her if that was okay to which she replied "Sure." At that point he told her that he needed her to pull down her blouse a little bit. Then it was a little more until she was topless and his camera was automatically clicking from every angle.

Samantha was a little uncomfortable with the situation but he kept telling her how beautiful she looked and those photos would be perfect for the European magazines. Then it was getting late and he told her he had to take her back home. He assured her that she did great and had a sensual appearance that made her exceptionally photogenic. She enjoyed all the flattery and began to think that maybe she had some type of special chemistry that would propel her desire to become an actress. Upon arriving at home, she got out of his car and walked into the house. She thought to herself how much more knowledgeable she was. At least she had learned the meaning of the 'European Look'.

She soon forgot about this slightly uncomfortable experience until her mother told her that Mr. Polanski wanted to pick her up for another photo shoot on Tuesday, May 10, 1977. Samantha hadn't said anything about the first photo shoot since she figured it was a onetime event. Her mother seemed excited for her to have another chance to work with such a famous person in the entertainment industry. So Sam, as her friends called her, got herself ready.

Polanski drove up in a classy Mercedes and she went out and jumped in and they took off. He explained that because of the lighting he wanted to get some shots up on top of the hills. He drove her up the hills to Mulholland Drive and she noticed all the luxurious estates. He graciously narrated like a tour guide which movie stars lived in which houses. As he neared a big bend in the road he said this was where Marlon Brando lived. He pulled into the driveway and exclaimed that Jack Nicholson lived in the house next door. He pressed in the security code and the tall iron gates creaked as they slithered open and he gunned the engine of the Mercedes as it maneuvered the curvy driveway.

Polanski uttered something about Jack being away and they could use his place for the photo shoot. They were met at the door by a lady who welcomed them in and said that she was finishing up something and was about to leave. What an awesome experience for a 13 year old girl to walk through the living room of one of the top actors in the world. She was impressed by all the awards and plaques filling the many shelves. Little Sam was all eyes taking it all in while Polanski was digging into his camera satchel. He was fiddling with lenses and some lighting equipment preparing for the Vogue magazine photo shoot.

CHAPTER 40 LOOSING UP FOR PHOTO SHOOT

Then he announced he was ready to start taking photos. He went through some background by saying that this was for the French Vogue magazine and naturally she needed to take her blouse off. Sam started having a creepy feeling but that was overcome when Polanski started pouring champagne in two glasses. He offered one glass to her and she momentarily hesitated but she thought to herself that maybe this was how adult photo shoots were conducted.

Unexpectedly she reached out and took the glass. As he held up his glass and started drinking, she found herself doing the same. The taste of the champagne was bitter but the bubbles tickled her nose. He smiled as she downed her champagne. Within seconds he was like a high paid bartender filling her empty glass. She wondered how a 13 year old girl was supposed to act in such a setting. She wanted to appear sophisticated; however, she didn't know what she should do. He said, "Bottoms up" and he downed another glass.

Her immediate thought was to do the same and she sipped her drink until it was empty. Within 15 to 20 minutes the champagne started to take its effect and the mood was somewhat mellow. He had been successful in convincing her to take her blouse off. He picked up the camera and it started clicking as he moved around to get various positions. Then she noticed that he put the camera down and went to an adjoining bathroom. The next thing she remembered was he had some type of capsule that he pulled apart with white powder that he held in his cupped hand.

He told her to try it. He claimed that it would relax her so they could get even better photos. All Sam remembered was feeling very high and not finding the word 'No'. She took the white powder and washed it down with more champagne.

Within minutes he suggested that they go outside to Jack's party size Jacuzzi. She was impressed with the gorgeous view of the city. Since the Jacuzzi was already warmed up, he told her to get in. As she was about to climb in he told her to take off her shorts and underwear. He said something about not getting her clothes wet. With all the champagne and the drugs that she had taken, this seemed to make sense to her. She discreetly turned around out of his view and removed her shorts and with a quick motion plunged into the Jacuzzi.

Now she was entirely naked in the Jacuzzi completely covered by the water. She laid back, feeling the water jets blowing warm water, massaging her 13 year old body. In order to complete the mood, the music to the outdoor speakers was turned on. Possibly the music included the top hit for 1977 which was ***Tonight's the Night-Gonna Be Alright*** by Rod Stewart. Polanski certainly was hoping that this night was going to be alright for him. However, there were other hits from the year that the young girl would be familiar with such as, ***I Just Want to Be Your Everything*** by Andy Gibb and possibly ***Dancing Queen*** of course by ABBA. ***Hotel California*** by the

Eagles may not have been the type of music needed to create a romantic atmosphere Polanski was looking for.

As she reclined in the tepid Jacuzzi she had never felt that relaxed. Her attention was directed at the view of the city and trying to identify various buildings and freeways that she was familiar with. Hearing some sounds of a closing door, she glanced over to her side. There she saw Polanski without any clothes on climbing into the Jacuzzi with her. This was unexpected since she had thought he was interested in getting her relaxed for special photos of her in the Jacuzzi. Then the next thing she realized was him trying to slide closer to her on the Jacuzzi bench.

Her immediate response was, "No, no, I've got to get out." He took his arms and grabbed her around the narrow of her waist. His hands began to do a touchy feely all over her nude body. She didn't know how to react. The champagne and the drugs had weakened her resistance. However, she was scared in that she was all alone and didn't know how to respond. Sam was a precocious 13 year old who had fooled around with her boyfriend. She had had some experimental sexual intercourse with someone her own age. However, she was unprepared to know how to act when an adult was involved.

It was a situation of 'What do I do now, Coach?' All she could think about was getting out of the Jacuzzi. Even with all the champagne and drugs she was able to come up with an excuse. She told him that she had asthma and the hot steam from the Jacuzzi was making it hard for her to breath. She got out of the Jacuzzi and went to the nearby bathroom and dried herself off. She put on her shorts and told him that she had to go.

CHAPTER 41 DOES "NO" MEAN "YES" IN POLANSKI'S WORLD?

His response was telling her to go into the bedroom and lay down and her asthma would be OK. She walked to the bedroom and sat on the side of the bed. He came up next to her and sat down. He leaned over and started kissing her. She said, "No, keep away." The next thing she noticed was that his head slid downward and then he was kissing her vagina area.

At that point she didn't know what to say or do. The best she could come up with was saying, "No. Come on stop it." Nothing was discouraging his conduct. He started to gently pull her shorts off completely and pushing her back to lay down on the bed. His nude body was stretched over her small torso. Then he slowly attempted to have sexual intercourse on her. As he moved back and forth over her body all she could think of was how to survive through this ordeal. She didn't want to say anything that would aggravate the situation.

He gently took his hand to pull her hair back from her eyes. As his hand moved down to her breast she immediately exclaimed, "No, No please." Then he in a hushed voice asked her, "Are you taking the Pill?" Samantha felt a tug-a-war going on within her body. She didn't know how to respond since she was now completely over her head. With a shaky voice she responded, "No I'm not on the Pill." And she figured that would end the unwanted intercourse. His follow up question was, "When was your last period?" Again she didn't know how to answer him.

To her surprise Polanski said, "That's OK. Would you want me go through your back?" She didn't seem to understand what was meant. She uttered the word, "No." But for whatever reason he began having anal sex with her. For over an hour he continued to engage in various forms sexual activity with her in countless positions that no 13 year old had heard of or could have imagined. Samantha didn't know how to react so she didn't say a word. She was truly terrified and didn't resist his advances.

He continued to reassure her that she would be OK. Throughout the ordeal he told her how beautiful she was and how happy she made him. She realized that if she played along with him she wouldn't be physically harmed. It was just a matter of time for all of this to end. Eventually, the alcohol and the drugs started wearing off and she realized she was in a situation she had never experienced before. How should she react in order to get him to take her home? What was she going to tell her mother?

Eventually he seemed to be tired out and laid on the bed looking at her. There was a broad smile on his face and he said, "We got to get you home." Then with a satisfied voice he said, "Don't tell anyone what we did here. Let this be our little secret." He stressed the importance not to tell anyone since they wouldn't understand. With a shy smile, she assured him that she wouldn't tell anyone.

As they were driving back to her house, Polanski uttered these words to Sam, "You know when I first met you I promised myself I wouldn't do anything like this with you." Sam had to wonder why he would say such a thing. He made it sound like it wasn't his fault in that it was the devil that made him do it. He was fighting the temptation but was overcome by evil forces.

He thanked her for the enjoyable time and said, "Good-bye." Sam turned away as he quickly exited her driveway. She sighed to herself and walked into her house. Those inside were curious about her afternoon with Mr. Polanski. Her response was non-descript as though it was just another modeling job. She went to her room to reflect and concentrate on what had happened to her and what to say and do. Her sister came in to interrogate her as to the details. Sam wondered how much she could tell without anyone learning about what she had just gone through. She did a little bragging to her sister by telling her how she had visited Jack Nicholson's house. She tried to distance herself from revealing any more details.

Sometime later she got on the phone with her boyfriend and started talking about their mutual friends. She might have been concerned about getting pregnant or some of the various sexual acts she had learned and experienced. She was trying to impress her boyfriend and started throwing out various sexual terms. She knew that she could trust her boyfriend because they had their own secrets that her mother didn't know about.

What Sam didn't realize was that her noisy sister was listening in on the private but revealing conversation she was having with her boyfriend. Her sister was absorbing every word of what she was explaining to her boyfriend. Her sister couldn't believe all the talk of sexual activity she was hearing. It didn't take long before she realized she was talking about her so called 'photo shoot' with Mr. Polanski.

CHAPTER 42

REVEALING THEIR SECRET

It wasn't clear whether Sam's sister was trying to get Sam in trouble or trying to protect her. Her sister couldn't contain herself as she started revealing to their mother what she had overheard. Their mother listened and at first she was in disbelief. She was skeptical thinking these are teenage girls with active imaginations. But as more sexual details were revealed their mother realized she needed to talk face to face with Sam immediately.

She went to look for Sam and when she found her she escorted her into a private room and closed the door. Then the mother daughter interrogation began. At first Sam didn't know where her mother had learned all the lured details of the photo shoot with Mr. Polanski. She didn't know what to say since she had promised Mr. Polanski that she wouldn't tell her mother. This was becoming an awkward moment for her and she started with denials. Yet her mother somehow knew about the sexual acts.

As the two were nearly in tears, Sam decided to disclose everything that occurred. As she gave more details about the various sexual acts her mother's blood pressure seemed to go up. Her mother's voice was becoming sterner and louder to the point that Sam had never seen her mother this upset.

Her mother then seemed to switch from interrogating to becoming more sympathetic as to what should be done next. It wasn't long before her mother was on the phone to the police department and from that moment on the world began to swing out of control.

Sam was required to talk to a rape sexual assault detective. Once the police realized who the suspect was, the question was asked as to whether they wanted a police report taken on this incident. When the location of the crime scene was determined to be Jack Nicolson's Mulholland address, the next question was whether the mother really wanted to pursue it. Sam didn't want the matter to be blown out of proportion. She wasn't forcibly harmed. Although she said, "No," she didn't do much in the way as to resistance.

Even when the detectives asked Sam's mother why she allowed her 13 year old daughter to go alone on a photo shoot, she didn't seem to understand the insinuation. She just became more incensed that Mr. Polanski would violate the trust in which she had allowed Sam to go with him. She wanted Polanski to be punished for taking advantage of Sam and her trust. When the detectives asked, "Are you sure you want to press charges against Mr. Polanski?" Sam's mother was absolute and there was no way she was going to let him get away with what he did to her daughter.

The detectives collected Sam's panties to check for semen. They then obtained a search warrant for where Mr. Polanski was living. Since he was staying in a hotel they got the search warrant for his room. There they found a number of Quaalude capsules and when they checked his camera they discovered photos of Sam without clothes on. All of these items corroborated what Sam had told the detectives.

When Mr. Polanski was contacted by the police, they talked through his attorney who indicated that he was a victim of a 'Casting Couch Extortion' by Sam's mother. Polanski's attorney claimed the mother was out to extract money from him. Her young daughter had been used as bait to set up the extortion.

The police took this 'hot potato' to the DA's Office. Prosecutors have been burned so many times that they are suspicious of these types of situations. If they file charges, by the time they get to trial all of a sudden the victim wants the charges dropped. By that time, the victim has been paid off or somehow accommodated. At time of trial, the prosecutor doesn't have a willing victim. The victim may have changed her story or states it was a mere misunderstanding. What the DA's Office ends up with is a dismissed case or a not guilty case after spending considerable time preparing these criminal charges.

When the LAPD Sexual Assault detective brought this case to the DA's Office it was looked at with a skeptical eye. The mother was adamant that she wanted criminal charges filed. The DA's said OK, we will send it to the Grand Jury for them to decide. At the grand jury preceding the prosecutor calls witnesses without the defendant or his or her attorney being present. The grand jury listens to the testimony and decides if there is enough evidence to indict the suspect. A detective testified that they found photos of the victim in Polanski's camera. The prosecutor called the forensic witness who verified that there was semen on the victim's shorts. (This occurred before DNA was used as a forensic tool.)

The grand jury considered all the evidence and decided to indict Mr. Roman Polanski of Furnishing Drugs to a Minor; Commit Lewd or Lascivious Act upon a Child Under Fourteen; Unlawful Sexual Intercourse; Rape by Use of Drugs; Perversion (Oral Copulation); and Sodomy on a Person. Many may criticize the DA's Office for using the Grand Jury to decide whether to charge Polanski. Many defense attorneys claim it is easy to get a Grand Jury to indict just about anyone. The saying goes that "A Grand Jury would even indict a cheese sandwich."

As soon as the indictment was filed, an arrest warrant was issued for Roman Polanski. Within a short time he was arrested and his mug shot was released for the entire world to see.

CHAPTER 43 WHO IS ROMAN POLANSKI?

Few human beings on the face of this earth have had such a horrific life as Roman Polanski. To begin with, he was born on August 18, 1933, in Paris, France and was given the name Rajmund Roman Liebling. He was truly a muddled mixture with a father who was a Polish Jew while his mother was a Russian Catholic. In 1937, his family migrated to Poland where his father became involved in paint and plastic manufacturing.

Roman's life was good for him until the Nazi-Soviet Pact which permitted Poland to be occupied by the Germans. Since his family identified with the Jews, they were forced to move into the Krakow Ghetto. As time went by, the persecution of the Jews became more dominant. His mother was apprehended and shipped to Auschwitz Concentration Camp where she died. At the same time his father was taken to an Austrian Concentration Camp where he was barely able to survive.

Roman was almost ten years old when his parents were taken away. Luckily for him, he must have had an archangel looking down on him. He was able to escape the Warsaw area and traveled to the countryside. There, he fortunately met a Polish Catholic farm family who were willing to shelter him as part of their clan. Their charitable support definitely saved his life so he didn't end up in one of the many concentration camps.

After the war he was 12 and his education took many twists and turns. During this time he had the opportunity to learn six languages and eventually became fluent in all of them. What distinguished him from all the other boys his age was his short stature. As he grew to manhood he never was taller than 5' 4." Whether his shortness created a Napoleonic complex in him is not known, but he was a person who was confident, if not cocky, in his view of himself. It wasn't until the mid-1950's did he attend the Polish Film School in Lodz, Poland. That experience changed his life. He had a sixth sense in knowing how to present a story in film. He demonstrated an uncanny ability to write, direct, and even act in his movies.

His first movie was titled ***When Angels Fall*** starring the young actress Barbara Lass. It wasn't a smash success but he came away as a winner in learning so much about filmmaking. The other thing he accomplished was marrying the incredibly beautiful star of the film, who was merely 15 years old. (His fondness for young girls started early on.)

Polanski went on to produce and direct what were considered eccentric edgy movies. First of the three was the ***Knife in the Water*** in 1962; ***Repulsion*** with Catherine Deneuve in 1965; and finally ***Dul-de-sac*** in 1966. He attracted an audience that liked movies that had a dark side to them.

Then in 1967, he became involved with the film ***The Fearless Vampire Killers***, starring Sharon Tate. Polanski was totally immersed in this film by being the director, producer, writer, as well as an actor in this movie. It was a comedy combined with a horror movie and he wanted certain actors and actresses that he could mold into the various characters. The studio wanted him to use Sharon Tate as the lead actress. He objected and didn't think she was right for the part. Polanski and the studio executives continued to disagree until finally he was given an ultimatum to use Sharon Tate, or there would be no funding for the movie.

Polanski was irate but agreed to use Sharon Tate. Begrudgingly, he started to work with her and it wasn't long before Polanski's objections to her melted away and he spent much of his time socializing with her. The rest is history, in that they became an inseparable couple who eventually married in London on January 25, 1968.

His career took an upward spiral in which he became well recognized for his incredible film making talents. The Hollywood studios wanted to use him on their 'new phase' of movies. Paramount Pictures Studio persuaded him in 1968 to move to Hollywood to start filming ***Rosemary's Baby.*** Without a doubt, this movie is considered by many to be one of the most eccentric movies ever made. It involved a character named Rosemary played by Mia Farrow who believed that the child she was pregnant with was the son of Satan. Polanski conveys a strange vision of evil. As a movie, it turned out to be a successful movie that received considerable attention.

When Polanski and his wife, Sharon Tate, moved to Hollywood they needed to find a comfortable house to live in. The word was out that Terry Melcher and Candice Bergan were moving out of a 'Ranch style' house above Beverly Hills which had a spectacular view of the city. Polanski's real estate agent showed the property to them and they were impressed and since it was vacant, they could move in immediately.

What they didn't realize was that Charlie Manson was familiar with the house since he had several musical jam sessions at that house with Terry Melcher. At that time, Manson was attempting to start a race war called Helter Skelter. Since he was acquainted with the old Melcher house, he decided to use it in his first attack. On August 9, 1969, the Manson family broke into the house where they encountered a new resident, that being Sharon Tate who was eight months pregnant. Others in the house were her friends who were spending the night with Sharon. On this warm summer night members of the Manson family brutally shot or stabbed all of them to death.

The only reason that Roman Polanski was spared was the fact that he was in Europe scouting new locations for a movie. Eventually, the murderers, Tex Watson, Susan Atkins, Patricia Krenwinkel, and Linda VanHouten were found guilty. Charles Manson who was the master mind of the murder plan was also convicted of the murders even though he didn't participate in the actual killings.

Polanski was devastated losing his lovely wife and unborn child. The fact is that if he had been at the house he would have likewise been killed. His personal tragedy seemed to play out in his next movie ***Macbeth*** in 1971. It was an especially bloody and gruesome depiction of Shakespeare's famous character. Some believed that Polanski's experience with the Manson killings affected him in the manner he told the story of Macbeth.

Three years later in 1974, he joined up with Jack Nicholson to direct ***Chinatown*** with Faye Dunaway. This was a highly successful movie in which Polanski appeared very briefly in the film in which he is the person who took a knife and slit Jack Nicholson's character's nose. If the two men hadn't become such close friends in this movie, then this child rape case wouldn't have occurred where it did up on Mulholland Drive.

CHAPTER 44 POLICE INVESTIGATION & DA CHARGING

The victim's family was not prepared for what was about to happen to them. It was like a ton of bricks that fell on top of them. Polanski, with his attorneys and the entire entertainment industry, condemned and accused the victim's mother of trying to extort money from Mr. Polanski. They claimed she had used her daughter as the lure.

The media started attacking the mother's character by asking what type of mother would let her 13 year daughter go with a man on a photo shoot. Every mother was shaking their head that no way would they have permitted their daughter to go on such a photo shoot. Sam's mother certainly wasn't going to be nominated as the 'Mother of the Year.' But the media was spinning the story in such a way that only a conniving mother would have agreed to such a photo shoot. It was alleged that she was motivated by the fact that she could extort money from a wealthy celebrity. The distain that the entire community had for Sam's mother was devastating.

In addition, Sam found that at school she was made fun of as though she was part of a conspiracy to extort money from one of the top directors in Hollywood. Her friends and fellow students looked upon her as a young Lolita who was attempting to seduce a vulnerable Polanski.

After several weeks of unrelenting pressure from the media and the community, Sam's family wanted to claim 'King's X' and do whatever was necessary to end this humiliation that they had brought upon themselves. They hired an attorney to file a motion to prevent Sam from being subpoenaed for trial. The family said to the court that they wouldn't permit their daughter to testify in the Polanski case. They claimed that such a court appearance would be psychologically damaging to her.

This placed the DA's Office in a difficult situation since they can't proceed against a defendant unless they know they have sufficient evidence to convict. Roger Gunson, who was the prosecutor assigned to the case, still maintained that they could continue to proceed with the case although they would have a hostile victim. The theory was that the DA was prosecuting a crime which was committed against the State and the individual victim had no legal standing to object to testifying in court. Even though the DA doesn't have to listen to the wishes of the victim, practically every prosecutor will consider the concerns of the victim.

In other words, the prosecutor was going to listen to Sam and her mother. However, the prosecution recognized that there were numerous Victim Rape groups who would be opposed to any dropping of charges. The pressure wasn't merely on

Sam's family but the DA's Office was bristling from public pressure from the anti-pedophile groups who wanted the case to be vigorously prosecuted.

Conversely, at the same time Roman Polanski and his attorney knew that his movie career would be over if the public became aware of the graphic details of sexual acts he committed against a 13 year old girl. Both sides didn't want to go to trial in this case. Both sides had too much to lose. The question was could any type of plea bargain be hammered out that would be acceptable to both sides.

CHAPTER 45 IS IT TIME FOR A PLEA BARGAIN?

The American Criminal Justice System receives considerable criticism when the prosecution and the defense attorneys try to work out some type of compromise in which both sides give something up to gain something. The courts have disliked using the term 'plea bargain' since it congers up the idea of a bargain like a K-Mart Blue Light Special. The more acceptable description is calling it a 'Case Settlement.'

American courts have never been given the luxury of having sufficient courtrooms to be able to try all cases that have been filed with the court. In order to actually try each and every felony case before a jury, each case would average four days. However, if a case can be settled without a trial, it may take less than an hour. The bottom line is that if the criminal justice system is to function with the limited number of courtrooms, then a large number of the cases need to be resolved without a jury trial.

The DA's Office is very much aware that the prosecution needs to prove the case beyond any 'reasonable doubt'. Everyone's threshold for some type of 'reasonable doubt' is different for all people. But the prosecution has to convince all 12 jurors that there is no 'reasonable doubt.' That is a high burden for the prosecution to meet. In other words, there is always some uncertainty whether 12 jurors will be willing to convict.

However, every prosecutor is faced with the real situation that he or she has to get through the day so every case by the end of the day is handled. A defendant has a right to a 'Speedy Trial' so the DA can't continue cases indefinitely. At the end of the each day, the court calendar of cases has to be somehow resolved. That may require the DA giving up something to move the cases.

Certain cases generate additional pressure on the DA not to settle the case. High profile cases can be a problem since the media will be reporting on any disposition. Cases involving children or animals have support groups that will put pressure on the DA not to dispose of their type of cases. These groups will want the defendant to receive the harshest punishment (maximum sentence). Any case settlement is looked upon as a sell out to the enemy. Then these groups will claim that the DA is 'Soft on Crime' which will come back to haunt the County District Attorney at election time.

Since the Roman Polanski case involved child sexual abuse, the Protection of Our Children groups were ready to demand the maximum sentence. These groups aren't interested in hearing about the difficulties in proving the case since their main interest is to apply pressure to the courts.

However, the Polanski case presented the DA's Office with a legitimate concern whether they would be able to convince a jury to convict Polanski. There were many factors that favored Polanski. First factor was the obvious one which was that everyone knew that Roman Polanski suffered the most horrific situation that anyone could face. His charming wife, Sharon Tate, was brutally murdered as well as his unborn son who was slaughtered by the Manson Family in 1969. If that wasn't sufficient tragedies in his life, he had to endure the Nazi takeover of the Polish ghetto which resulted in his parents being sent to concentration camps. There, his mother was exterminated and his father was barely able to survive.

After such a tragic childhood he went on to study film making and demonstrated his talents to be one of the top film makers in America. All his life he had been law abiding with no criminal record of any type.

Some of the issues that the Defense had going for it was the fact that there was the appearance that Polanski was being set up. There was the claim made by Polanski's supporters that the victim's mother was trying to extort money from Polanski. The argument implied that Sam's mother wanted to be an actress and understood how the 'Casting Couch' concept worked and she was willing to sacrifice her daughter to be in a position to gain financially.

The victim's mother was easy to ridicule since she was more than willing to have her 13 year old daughter go alone to a photo shoot without any adult supervision. The media's claim was what mother would have permitted their daughter to be made the sacrificial lamb? There were many who thought that Polanski did nothing wrong but was set up by a crafty woman.

Other people have a more laid back European view that young girls don't need to be protected. They believe that young teenage females are going to attract the attention of men. Their belief is that it is a natural way females learn about sex. What we know from the facts was that the victim had been having sexual intercourse with her boyfriend. She wasn't unfamiliar with sexual intercourse. The more liberal European approach would emphasize that the victim wasn't forced to submit to these sexual acts in that she didn't vigorously object but gave a tacit consent.

There were some who felt that Polanski was effected by the alcohol and drugs and wasn't showing good judgment when he committed the sexual acts. All of these were factors that could create sympathy for Polanski and disdain for the victim and her mother.

The DA knew that all of these factors would influence jurors as to whether they would convict Polanski of the felony charges. All of these problems with the case were being heaped on the fact that the victim's family stated that they wouldn't permit her to testify in court. Without the victim's testimony, there was no way Polanski would be convicted. Ethically, the DA shouldn't continue with a case if he or she knows there isn't sufficient evidence to obtain a conviction. The DA's Office went on the assumption that somehow the victim would be persuaded to take the witness stand coupled with the naked photos of the victim found on Polanski's camera.

The prosecutor wasn't holding any Aces but neither was the Defense. Roman Polanski couldn't afford to have the public learn about the erotic acts he perpetrated on a 13 year old girl. If it had been merely some inappropriate touching in the Jacuzzi, his career wouldn't have been impacted. But all the sexual acts he committed on her were going to turn off any studio from ever dealing with him in the future. His film making career was going to come to an end if somehow the DA were able to have the victim testify in open court. Although the Defense had the better set of cards, the Defense under no conditions wanted to play its hand of cards.

CHAPTER 46 THE SENTENCING IS UNRAVELING

With so much pressure on both sides it was understandable that a case settlement was hammered out in which both sides got something they wanted. The DA agreed that Polanski could plead guilty to having **unlawful sexual intercourse with a minor** and at time of sentencing, all the other felonies would be dismissed against Polanski. The sentencing would be left up to the judge to decide. However, in the meantime, the defendant would be sent to Chino State Prison for a 90 day CDC (California Department Corrections) Diagnosis Study.

Both sides seemed to have negotiated the Case Settlement mine field without anything blowing up. The prosecutor, Roger Gunson, got a conviction to a felony related to child sexual abuse. The Defense attorney prevented a trial in which the child victim would have testified. He was able to keep a lid on a volatile situation. All he had to do was work out a time for Polanski to surrender to the state prison in Chino. Since Polanski was finishing up a movie in Europe, the judge gave him time to conclude the filming and then report to state prison.

For years the DA's Office had used the 90 day State Prison Diagnostic Study as a way to get the attention of neophyte criminals. There is something therapeutic about living in a prison for 90 days that makes a positive impression on a person from the clanging of prison doors; maybe it is the baloney sandwiches for lunch; sharing a cell with Bobo; or the hard and cold concrete bunk beds. After a 90 day stay at a prison facility, most people come to the realization that they are willing to agree to any type of conditions for probation as long as they don't have to return to serve time in prison.

Polanski was the perfect candidate for the 90 day Diagnostic Study. Remember, he was used to living in the finest homes in Hollywood and staying at five star hotels when he was away from home. Polanski would have 90 nights lying in his bunk reflecting on the wisdom of having sex with minors. Most people would think that the 90 day stay in state prison would act as a deterrent in changing a person's errant ways.

Everything was agreed to for Polanski spending his time in Chino State Prison. It was unclear how he would spend his days in prison since he could have been making license plates or binding school text books. Or possibly he could be assigned to do 'sparkle duty' to clean the latrines or working in the prison laundry.

However, for some unexplainable reason Polanski was released from Chino State Prison after serving only **47 days**. Possibly he was a model prisoner or the Diagnostic Program had run out of spaces. Or, could it be that somehow he received preferential treatment with his attorney's help. Or possibly someone at the prison might have felt sorry for him. No one is talking as to why Polanski got a break and was released early.

When the DA's Office found out about the early release it tried to find out why. The entire idea of sending a person on a 90 day Diagnostic was for them to realize they don't want to be sentenced to State Prison. When Judge Rittenband found out that Polanski spent less than half the time at Chino, he was livid. For him, when he sent a defendant to serve 90 days he meant 90 days and certainly not half of it.

Later, there were allegations that a member of the DA's Office had a conversation with the judge about the 47 day stay at the State Prison. There were some allegations in which a rouge prosecutor talked to the judge and encouraged the judge to throw the book at Polanski. That would be certainly improper if Polanski's attorney wasn't present. However, that allegation sidesteps the main issue.

The main concern was who told Polanski that the judge was furious at his special treatment and was considering sentencing Polanski to state prison and afterwards having him deported from the country. Since the time of the plea, the public was speculating what the judge would do at time of sentencing. The Women's and Child Abuse groups were rallying to impose a harsh sentence for what they considered the repugnant crimes Polanski had committed. The judge may have had buyer's remorse and felt the pressure to appear tougher on child sex molesters. That may explain why the judge was having second thoughts about a light weight sentence for Polanski.

No one knows for sure how Polanski found out that the judge was considering a harsher sentence for him. Apparently, the 47 days staying at state Prison had convinced Polanski that he didn't want to spend several years in the 'Big House.' Most likely his Defense attorney may have tipped Polanski off that things weren't looking good for him. His attorney denies informing Polanski that the judge was going to throw the book at him.

What we do know, as a fact, was that Roman Polanski on February 1, 1978, was on a one way flight to Paris, France. He knew that France would not extradite him back to the USA on the charge of Unlawful Sexual Intercourse on a Minor. Several European countries take a much more liberal position on such cases. They considered the charge to be no more than a misdemeanor on which they would not extradite.

If only someone back in 1978 could have figured out a way for Polanski to finish up the 43 more days, this international incident wouldn't have ever occurred. The DA and the judge would have had to abide by the original agreement which would have given Polanski some type of probationary sentence. If only Polanski wouldn't have been released early he most likely would have become America's greatest director of all times.

CHAPTER 47 THE NEW FUGITIVE

When the news broke that Polanski had split the country, most people thought that this case couldn't become anymore bizarre. Now Roman Polanski was on the lamb. He became America's real life 'Fugitive' on February 1, 1978 when a new warrant was issued for his arrest. Between 1963 and1967, there was a TV program named the ***Fugitive*** in which David Janssen played the part of Dr. Richard Kimble who was arrested for the murder of his wife in their home. He wasn't the true killer but he had seen a one armed man leaving the murder scene but no one believed him. Later he escaped and tried to catch his wife's real killer without himself being caught. From that point on, Dr. Kimble became the FUGITIVE.

In 1993, the ***Fugitive*** movie was made starring Harrison Ford which was a popular thriller film. Polanski's role as a Fugitive was different in that he wasn't an innocent man running from the law in order to catch the real criminal. Yet, Polanski certainly lived the role of the Fugitive longer than David Janssen and Harrison Ford played the part. He has been able to continue as a Fugitive for over 35 years. The other difference was that Polanski didn't have to hide from law enforcement. He could work and live in the open as long as he didn't travel to certain countries that would be willing to extradite him back to the USA.

Since the French authorities would not arrest him, he was able to carry on his life as a film director. In1979, he did an adaption of Thomas Hardy's novel ***Tess*** of the D'Urbervilles featuring Nastassja Kinski, playing a young peasant whose chances of happiness are thwarted by a series of unfortunate twists of fate and repressive Victorian morality of the time. He dedicated the film to his murdered wife, Sharon Tate, who was the one who had encouraged him to tell the story. The movie turned out to be successful and won three Academy Awards. Since he was a Fugitive from the USA, he was unable to receive any of the Oscars at the Hollywood ceremony.

Life went on for Roman Polanski and in 1987, he directed a movie titled ***Frantic***, starring Harrison Ford. (Six years later, Harrison Ford starred in the movie ***Fugitive).*** While making this movie, Polanski met and worked with the co-star, Emmanuelle Seigner, who was a French fashion model, actress, and singer. They spent considerable time together getting to know each other. Although she was considerably younger than he was, they married in 1989.

In order to put things in perspective, his young wife was only three years old when Sharon Tate was murdered. She would have been only 11 years old when Polanski was charged with rape of the 13 year old victim. She was unaware of so many of the other things that had occurred in Polanski's life. Their marriage produced a son and a daughter. She continued to make other movies such as ***Bittermoon*** in 1992, and ***The Ninth Gate*** in 1999.

Then in 2001, Polanski directed the movie ***Pianist*** which paralleled his own life to some extent. It was a story about a brilliant pianist, a Polish Jew, who witnessed the

Nazi's placing restrictions on the Jewish people living in the Warsaw ghetto. As the pianist's family is rounded up and shipped off to Nazi labor camps, he is able to escape deportation by living in the ruins of Warsaw. This character, who is the pianist, is a witness to the notorious Warsaw Ghetto Uprisings.

As much as this movie meant to Polanski, he was unable to go to Hollywood to receive the Academy Award for this highly acclaimed movie. He had to have a Mr. Ronald Harwood accept the Oscar for him. One wonders what went through his mind when he sat in his home in France and saw someone else receive the coveted award on his behalf when he should have been present to enjoy all the accolades and fanfare. What a price to pay to miss one of the paramount moments in his career.

CHAPTER 48 THE CAT AND MOUSE GAME

Roman Polanski has gone down in history as one of the longest running 'Fugitive.' This most likely isn't the way he would like to be remembered. The question remains why hasn't the USA, a nation that prides itself as a super power, not been able to snare Polanski and bring him back to resolve his case. The irony is that America, as a nation, has proved it could capture some of the most wanted men in history. Saddam Hussein was found hiding in a hole in the ground and was captured by U.S. troops and later tried for his atrocities. Bin Laden seemed to be the most elusive man in history until Seal Team 6 tracked him down and terminated his reign of terror.

Why can't the most powerful nation capture Roman Polanski? He is entirely visible that everyone knows where he is. The answer has been that certain countries will extradite for special type of crimes and others will not. As stated earlier, France will not extradite a person for the crime of Unlawful Sexual Intercourse with a minor. As long as Polanski remains in sympathetic countries, he is safe from capture.

The next question is why hasn't Polanski been arrested when he has traveled to other countries that could extradite him but he is never picked up? It is well known that he has traveled to England and stayed there to do several motion pictures. The DA's Office has tried to extradite him from England but has not been successful based on several obstacles.

In order for an extradition to get started, some person or agency has to notify the DA's Office that Polanski is at a specific location. Then the DA's Office has to contact the foreign law enforcement agency to go out and verify that the fugitive is at the location. This is the tricky part. If the local law enforcement agency asks too many questions that often tips off the fugitive who immediately leaves that location.

In other words, the DA's Office is dependent on the local agency that doesn't have any 'Skin in the Game'. Local agencies don't want to spend resources chasing around a celebrity like Polanski who has the money to instantly move from place to place. Once the DA's Office is certain that Polanski is in the foreign country, it has to prepare a massive Extradition Package which includes certified documents including the charging complaint; the actual legislation making such offenses a crime; a list of the punishment for those crimes; Affidavit of Sheriff Deputy assigned the case; Affidavit of Deputy District Attorney; a photograph of the defendant; the transcript of the plea of Guilty to Unlawful Sexual Intercourse of a Minor, a felony; Court Dockets of court proceeding and the defendant's failure to appear; and the Warrant for the Arrest of the defendant.

When the Extradition Package has been completed, it must go on a cumbersome journey through numerous legal authorities. The following are the steps taken when

Polanski was thought to be in England. The DA's Office sends it to the Governor of California then to the U.S. State Department, passing through the Office of the President of the U.S.; then to the Queen of England where it is forward to the Ministry of Justice, and eventually assigned to some Bobbie to go out and arrest Polanski.

Just to illustrate how cumbersome the extradition process is, the APPLICATION FOR REQUISTION must contain the following worded document in order to extradite from the United Kingdom:

"To the Governor of the State of California,

I have the honor herewith to make application for requisition upon the Secretary of State of the United States to request the President of the United States to request of Her Majesty, the Queen of England, the arrest and rendition of Roman Raymond Polanski, who has pled guilty in this country to the crime of Unlawful Sexual Intercourse with a 13-year-old girl, a felony, and who failed to appear for sentence ...and is a fugitive from the justice of the State of California, United States of America, and has taken refuge in England."

Needless to say getting all the documents takes considerable time. The process is so time consuming since all the documents pass through and need to be approved by so many parties. The governor of the state has to review and approve the extradition then send to the U.S. Secretary of State for the president of the U.S., and to the head of the other country which could be the queen, president, or prime minister. At each step, the extradition can be held up by anyone of the parties who may have other priorities and not expedite the extradition arrest warrant.

It may take weeks or even months to get everyone to approve the extradition and by that time the fugitive has moved on to another location or country. In May of

1978, the DA's Office had received word Polanski was in England but by the time the paperwork was completed he was back in France where he was safe from extradition.

On one occasion the DA's Office heard Polanski was traveling to Brazil so an 'Extradition Packet' was created. However, when the fugitive goes to a non-English speaking country all the documents in the packet have to be translated into Portuguese. Of course, that takes considerable time since the DA's Office has to find a translator who can convert all the legalese into the other country's language. This all takes time and a high level of expertise. In Polanski's case, he was long gone from Brazil by the time all the documents arrived for his extradition.

There was another time when the DA's Office received an announcement that the Toronto International Film Festival was going to honor Polanski giving him a life time achievement award. The DA's Office (your author was in charge of the Extradition Unit and was the one to initiate this attempt to extradite Polanski) contacted the authorities in Canada to see if they would be willing to hold Polanski temporarily until we had all the documents prepared and go through the chain of command to their Prime Minister. The Mounties in Toronto were willing to detain him if we expedited the paperwork. The fact that Polanski would be able to bail out was recognized as a problem; however, it was still worth trying to extradite him since the entire case might be able to be finally resolved. When the plane landed in Toronto, the Mounties entered it and found no Roman Polanski. Somehow he must have been tipped off and never got on the flight. This ended up as one more missed opportunity to extradite the elusive Roman Polanski.

CHAPTER 49 HOW TO SOLVE THE UNSOLVABLE?

Over 35 years Polanski has remained on the run as the DA's Office has made numerous attempts to find a way to work out a solution. At times, Polanski, through his attorneys, has tried to resolve the situation so he can return to the USA. However, after the HBO program titled ***Roman Polanski Wanted and Desired*** which was shown on national television on June 8, 2008, there was a landslide of renewed interest in finding a resolution.

The HBO program included interviews with many of the key players; the film raises major questions about the workings of the US legal system and the media. It also examined the role of the various characters involved in the sentencing and legal proceedings. During the program DA, Roger Gunson, expressed some concerns about some of the court's actions as to whether the judge had changed his mind about the sentencing.

Polanski's attorney Douglas Dalton revealed some of the issues that occurred behind the scenes. The victim who was the woman at the center of the case, Samantha Geimer, clearly expressed her support for Roman Polanski. She even said during the HBO program that she wished her mother had never called the police in the first place.

What surprised most viewers of the HBO program was the fact that the victim appeared to want the DA's Office to stop chasing after Polanski. It was one of those idyllic moments in which the victim wanted everyone to forgive and forget. What the public didn't see was the landscape had changed over all these years. The victim had brought a civil lawsuit against Polanski and she successfully received a judgment against him. Her attorney went after the proceeds from Polanski's movies in order to collect on her judgment.

The victim was able to collect money that had been paid to Polanski in the USA. After a number of years, Polanski was having difficulty being paid for his movies. Eventually, Polanski's attorneys met with the victim's attorneys and a secret civil settlement was worked out. Only the two parties and their attorneys know the exact terms of the settlement. The reliable speculation was that the victim received an amount around $700,000. The other part of the bargain may have been that the victim would state that she wanted the charges to be dropped against Polanski. This latter part of the bargain could never be verified. However, Samantha Geimer, after the settlement, has become very vocal that the DA should stop pursuing Polanski since he has suffered enough.

In 2009, it was announced that the Swiss Film Festival in September was going to honor Roman Polanski for his significant contribution to film making. Since Polanski had a chalet in Switzerland, he felt comfortable leaving his home in Paris for a brief visit to Switzerland. On September 16, 2009, after 31 years on the run, he crossed over into Switzerland. In the computer system was the outstanding warrant for his arrest for the March 10, 1978 incident.

The Swiss authorities took him into custody. The USA agreed to send the extradition documents as soon as they were translated. He remained in jail for three months while the paperwork proceeded through channels. His attorneys asked the Swiss authorities to permit Polanski to be placed under House Arrest in his Swiss chalet that he owned. Since it appeared that the proceedings would take considerable time, the Swiss agreed that he remain at his chalet and not leave.

The legal battles occurred on two fronts. Originally Polanski brought an action in the Los Angeles Superior Court a 'Demand for Dismissal' of the case due to misconduct. His attorneys claimed that the judge had reneged on his agreement to sentence Polanski to probation. They wanted a hearing so they could call a former deputy district attorney to find out if he talked to the judge about sentencing. The argument against holding such a hearing was the fact that the defendant can't raise such an issue (as to alleged improper action by the judge and DA) until he surrenders to the court's jurisdiction. This put the Defense into a difficult position, since they didn't want him to surrender to the court until they knew for certain what his sentence would be.

The Catch 22 situation put Polanski in an untenable situation. Then his attorney started to try to negotiate as to what sentence Polanski would be willing to agree to. There was the possibility that he could be required to finish up his 90 day evaluation.

(Serve 43 days in the state prison). The other was to receive probation with an agreement to do Community Service, such as make some type of film about the court system.

Over a period of several months, there were two vocal groups that weighed in on the Polanski case. First, the sympathetic groups that said that he had suffered enough by not being permitted to return to America for over 30 years. Some of these groups stressed that the victim didn't want Polanski to suffer any more punishment. Then there were the stalwarts of the entertainment industry that pointed out what a major contribution he had made to film making.

On the other side were the child abuse advocate groups that thought that his behavior was so despicable that he was nothing short of a child molester and such persons should be prosecuted to the full extent of the law to protect the children of the world. These people wanted Polanski sent to state prison and later deported from the country.

The little country of Switzerland found itself in the middle of something they had not created. They had to get along with France, their neighbor to the north, whose premier had taken the side of their resident, Roman Polanski. European opinion was that poor little Switzerland shouldn't have to do the dirty work for the big bad USA. The Swiss court had to hold hearings on the extradition. The Swiss were hoping that the matter would be resolved in the hearings taking place in Los Angeles. But when the Los Angeles court denied the 'Hearing in Absentia', the Swiss court claimed that they would have to determine if there had been some type of misconduct on the part of the prosecutor and/ or judge.

The Swiss court asked for the transcript of the prosecutor's statements. The DA's Office explained that the transcripts had been already submitted to the Swiss court. Then one day in June of 2010, out of the blue, the Swiss court stated that they wouldn't extradite Polanski since they had not received a sealed transcript from the DA's Office.

Upon receiving word of Switzerland's refusal to extradite, Polanski immediately returned to France. The Swiss quietly washed their hands of the Polanski matter. The USA announced that the arrest warrant was still outstanding for Polanski and if he dare step his foot in the USA he would be immediately arrested.

Polanski's groups were ecstatic that he was released and could be back making movies and being with his young family. The Protect Our Children from Predators groups weren't happy that he was not extradited but they were pleased that the wicked 76 year old Roman Polanski would not be wandering the streets of America looking for young girls to molest.

After years of playing a 'Cat and Mouse Game', the extradition of Polanski is still pursued by the DA's Office whenever they receive word that he is traveling to other countries. Attempts have been made to his native Poland to extradite him. The Arrest Warrant is kept active in that if he ever came back to the USA, the Immigration authorities would arrest him. Also, the Arrest Warrant was given to Interpol so they could be notified if Polanski was moving from country to country. Over the past 35 years, there have been many attempts to apprehend Roman Polanski and bring him to justice. However, he has become the **'Teflon Fugitive'** who continues to wiggle his way out of being captured.

CHAPTER 50 LIFE GOES ON

Since all attempts to extradite Polanski seem to fail, his life has continued for all concerned. Polanski continues to make movies. His children continue growing up. He is still restricted where he can travel.

Samantha Geimer, the so called victim, is married with three children and lives in Hawaii. Whether it was only $700,000 or more that she was able to extract from Polanski, she seems to be living quite well. She has become a mini-celebrity partly due to her book about the incident.

The DA's Office has bigger fish to fry. However, the prosecutors are always mindful of the various women's and children's groups who want vigorous prosecution of Sex Offenders.

The DA's Office, in the Roman Polanski case, found itself in a no win situation. When the victims' parent's hired an attorney to make sure that the young girl would not testify in open court, the DA had a tough ethical decision. A prosecutor can't prosecute a case when the prosecutor knows there isn't sufficient evidence to support a conviction. Should a prosecutor continue to pursue a case even if the key witness refuses to testify? In the Polanski case, the prosecutor could claim the crime was committed against the State and it doesn't matter whether the victim wants to prosecute or not.

Another philosophic question is; how long should the DA's Office pursue a suspect to bring him or her to justice? As to charging suspects with crimes there is a statute of limitation that limits when charges can be filed. The rationale for the statute of limitation is that the police and prosecutor can't wait so long that the defendant can't find witnesses to mount a defense.
This rationale doesn't exist in a situation where the defendant knows he has been charged and voluntarily leaves the court's jurisdiction.

There are two schools of thought as to how long to pursue a fugitive. One is that we never forget. The logic is that anything less would be an incentive for defendants to not appear, stay away long enough, and then they get away with it.

The other approach is to weigh other factors and to give up at some point. What determines when to give up maybe the manner in which the defendant has lived his or her life on the run. Other factors to consider would be the victim's involved and how they have been compensated. In the Polanski case, his giving up the right to work and live in America for 35 years is certainly a high price that he has paid.

Every time the Polanski case is re-examined, one shakes one's head in wonderment as to how did we ever get to this impasse. Polanski was a stubborn individual from Poland who didn't trust the prosecution. The DA's Office didn't want to give a benefit to a person who had thumbed his nose at the American Judicial System. As we grow to maturity, we all experience impasses that can be easily solved but aren't because neither side wants to take a risk. The successful problem solvers are those who are willing to take a risk and then say, "It's time to move on."

In May of 2017, Polanski tried a new approach by hiring one of the venerable Defense attorneys Harland Braun to represent him in another attempt to resolve the matter. Braun brought the victim Smantha Geimer to court to ask that the case be finally dismissed against Polanski. She stated, "I have been serving a 40 year sentence, and I ask you to give me justice and relief as an act of mercy to myself and my family." The judge thanked her for her input but stated, "There is one person who "holds the key" to that closure: POLANSKI. If the director were to return to the U.S. for sentencing, that matter could be finished once and for all."

KILLERS ON MULHOLLAND DRIVE

(MURDER ON LOVER'S LANE)

CHAPTER 51 FRIDAY NIGHT ON LOVER'S LANE

It was a balmy Friday evening on October 17, 1997. At the end of a long week what would be better than going out for drinks and some dancing while enjoying a spectacular view with an attractive date. Nothing of great notoriety had occurred on the date of October 17 except in 1931. Al Capone was convicted of income tax evasion. Or, if one was looking for something upbeat, the news was that Mother Teresa had been awarded the Nobel Peace Prize on this date in 1979. But in Hollywood on this date in 1997, there wasn't anything special except the movie ***Titanic*** was still playing in some theaters. ***Titanic's*** worldwide gross had risen to $1,843,201,268. Other movies still showing in town were ***The Lost World of Jurassic Park*** and a few theaters still featured ***The Men in Black***.

Dario was 27 and had a good job with an armored car company and lived in the Burbank area. He had met **Hazel** who worked at one of the local banks. What they both had in common was that they both worked with lots of money. They had known each other for about three months and enjoyed each other's company. Like young working people they planned to get together late in the evening. Dario picked up Hazel around 10:45 p.m. in his Jeep Cherokee. Although some young women wouldn't be impressed being chauffeured about in a Jeep, but Hazel wasn't deterred by it. Dario took pride in polishing and making his Cherokee Jeep look presentable even if it wasn't a typical 'Datemobile.'

If Dario's Jeep wasn't going to amaze Hazel, at least he could take her to an impressive place. On the Westside of L.A., one sure place to impress a date was at Monty's Steakhouse in Westwood Village. It was located in the penthouse suite in the tallest building in the Village. From its location at night one could see the sparkling lights of Los Angeles. Nothing can be better than enjoying the incredible view while feasting on a tender, perfectly grilled steak.

This was a place that guaranteed a successful date; however, two steak dinners could be a little pricey. Not to imply that Dario was a little on the cheap side but he took Hazel there not for a steak dinner but for drinks and dancing. The results are the same without the $100 dinner tab. They hung out in the piano bar area where they could have a couple of drinks and relax on overstuffed chairs while gazing out at the dazzling city lights. When the dance floor thinned out, they took advantage of it.

Not to be melancholic, but from where they were seated on the top floor of this high rise, they could look down and see the Westwood Cemetery where Marilyn Monroe is entombed and Nathalie Wood is buried. That cemetery is the final resting place of so many famous celebrities. While glancing to the east one can view Beverly Hills where many movie stars call home.

Yet what mesmerizes most patrons is to stare out the large windows and see airplanes landing at LAX. It is ease to envy all those passengers flying in from some distant place around the world. Earlier in the afternoon the planes land approximately every minute but at this late hour the landings were less frequent.

As the evening approached midnight and the early morning hours begin, the traffic on the 405 Freeway thinned out and eventually the bartender was reminding the patrons that it was the last call for drinks. Just before closing, Dario and Hazel finished off their last drink and took the elevator all the way down to the parking garage. By 2:00 a.m., they drove slowly up Hilgard which is Sorority Row for the UCLA campus. They had to slow for all the cars double parked dropping off sorority girls who had to be in by 2:00 a.m. or they would be grounded for the next weekend. Dario maneuvered around the traffic and drove past the main buildings of the UCLA campus which looked so majestic at that late hour.

They weaved their way up to Sunset Boulevard where they turned to the right and drove for a few blocks until they reached Beverly Glen Boulevard, where they veered left up the hill. This is the main road that traverses the Santa Monica hills dividing Central Los Angeles from the San Fernando Valley. Most UCLA students are familiar with Beverly Glen since it can be a lifesaver when the main thoroughfare, the 405 Freeway, becomes a parking lot. Although Beverly Glen is curvy and narrow, at least it moves faster than the 405. (Why this is important in our story is Hazel later remembers that Dario mentioned to her that they were traveling on Beverly Glen. When they reached the summit he said let's see the lights along Mulholland Drive. This fact will be critical whether Hazel lives or dies.)

As Dario slowly drove the crest of the mountain range, there were spectacular vistas on both sides of the narrow road. During the early morning hours when traveling along Mulholland Drive, one feels a sense of floating along the top of the world. The city lights seem to extend into infinity like a twinkling tapestry. They drove by Mary Tyler Moore's estate on the San Fernando side then came upon Annette and Warren Beatty's impressive home. Driving around a bend they see the house lived in by Bruce Willis and Demi Moore, which is a reminder that not all marriages in Hollywood last forever.

Further along the road on the other side is a house or mini-mansion that has been home to two venerable movie stars starting with Ida Lupino and later it was home to Joan Fontaine. The next part of Mulholland Drive starts a gradual curve to the left. Dario wasn't aware that he was approaching 'Bad Boys Curve' (Homes of Marlon Brando and his neighbor Jack Nicholson) with the iron gate closed tightly not telling any stories that night. Dario, having negotiated the sharp curve, drove by the house that John Lennon once lived in. No question this road is paved with memories of bygone eras.

Dario continued driving looking for a turn out overlooking the Hollywood side of the mountain. He knew there were incredible views between Coldwater Canyon and Laurel Canyon. The first vista seemed a little crowded with two cars crammed into the little turn out. He slowed because he knew there was another spot further along Mulholland. As he came around a bend, he could see the turn out and there were no cars parked there.

He eased the Jeep off the pavement onto the dirt shoulder. It was a little bouncy as he maneuvered around ruts and some mini-boulders. He parked the Jeep so the windshield had a wraparound view of the city lights. He pointed out to Hazel how far they could see. Even the Los Angeles City Hall, the so called 'Pointee Building', was visible. At one time, the City Hall Building was the tallest structure in the city.

Since Los Angeles often experiences earthquakes it was thought that it was unsafe to have a building any higher than 32 floors (454 feet). In 1964, the city charter was amended so taller buildings were permitted to be built. Now there are many skyscrapers that dwarf the old city hall building.

It was a brisk October evening and the city lights were shimmering. By now it was 2:45 a.m. and most of the Hollywood's Lover's Lane visitors have moved on. What goes through a young couples mind with such an amazing panoramic view? Many guys think that someday they will make it big and they will be able to afford a home with such a view. From a woman's prospective, the view doesn't get much better than this. For many couples it is the place where sexual petting is anticipated but not to the extent requiring a motel room.

It was a perfect night and a perfect setting. Both Dario and Hazel were getting comfortable. They were safely parked on the side of Mulholland Drive and not bothering any of the celebrities who were tucked in bed in their palatial estates lining Mulholland Drive. Things couldn't be better for either Dario or Hazel. To set the mood, Dario turned on the radio and very likely listened to Elton John's big hit for 1997, *Candle in the Wind.* For over an hour they listened to the pop tunes like Whitney Houston's *I Believe in You and Me* and *Un-Break My Heart* by Toni Braxton

Both had heard about the tragic death of Ennis Cosby ten months earlier just off of Mulholland Drive. However, the thought of Ennis' death wasn't on either of their minds until they both noticed that two black men had gotten out of a car behind them. The men slowly approached the car, one remaining directly behind and one walking on the driver's side appearing to look into the tinted windows by tilting his head down as though he was trying to see inside the car. That man proceeded further to the front and continued to gaze at the car trying to look inside.

Hazel's memory, "...you could feel that something was going to happen, that's what I felt... we wanted to see what they were going to do...we thought...they definitely were going to do something." "Then the man in front of our car walked to the other side of the Mulholland Drive and pulled out a large .357 Magnum and again started approaching the car."

CHAPTER 52 WHAT'S GOING ON?

It had been a lovely evening with a full moon and an unbelievable view of the city below them. In an instant, Dario and Hazel were faced with a nightmare. They realized they were trapped in an enclosed car with a man approaching with a .357 Magnum and they both were frozen with fear. What should they do? Their minds tried to figure out what should they do to survive? One's first response is to be extremely quiet in hopes that these intruders will somehow go away. As Dario was watching the man approaching with the gun, he leaned slightly forward and turned the key to start the engine. Hazel could hear the muffled sound of the engine.

The gunman continued to approach the driver's side of the car and tapped the gun against the window and said, "Give me your money." Somehow Dario raised his hands and said "Okay, okay, okay." From that point in time, a chaotic situation occurred. Without rolling down the window Dario gradually slid his right hand to the shifter and placed the car in 'Drive.' What happened next was confusing. What was known for certain was that the gun was fired and a bullet struck Dario in the head next to his left ear causing him to suffer a gunshot wound. At the same time the Jeep accelerated forward.

Hazel, by this time, had ducked her head down toward Dario. After the first shot she remembers hearing squealing of tires causing road gravel to spray. At first the Jeep Cherokee didn't seem to be moving. Hazel with her head down couldn't see what was happening. However, her other senses could hear and feel the car moving over the gravel shoulder onto the solid asphalt road. The car seemed to be picking up speed as Dario's body leaned over onto Hazel with his foot pressing down on the accelerator. Then Hazel felt the car veer to the left and the car again hit the dirt shoulder on the other side of the the roadway.

Hazel raised her head slightly to see the car heading off the side of the road. At that moment she felt a sensation she had never experienced before as the car went airborne. It was a peculiar sensation since all of sudden it seemed completely silent. The car was gliding through the air like a soaring bird. Next, was the sensation of the car striking branches of trees and brush. Since it was dark out, Hazel couldn't see how steep the cliff was that she and the car flew over. Her ears hurt with the deafening sound of striking metal and the car windows breaking into shards of glass. Then she felt the car rolling over and over striking things that propelled it in a different direction. Hazel kept bouncing around inside the Cherokee. Several times Dario's body collided with hers as they tossed around like rag dolls.

Hazel wasn't aware of how far the car had rolled down the steep cliff. The car finally came to rest 170 feet below Mulholland Drive. Hazel was numb from all the noise of the car crashing and windows smashing. Her body felt bruised and broken. Dazed and disoriented, she wondered what to do next. There were more creaking noises as the car tried to find a stable resting place. Her senses were heightened by the dust and smells of a car turned upside down. The faint odor of gasoline became more pungent.

After several moments she started calling for Dario to make it all right. When she called his name, there was no answer. She could see part of his body in the back seat and the other portion was sticking outside the car. Was he knocked out or paralyzed from his injuries? As it became quieter, she came to the realization that she was stuck in a car that came to rest on the driver's side. The car was so crushed that she had no way of crawling out any of the windows or doors.

As time passed, her mind was absorbed by the fact that she thought the robbers were coming down the slope to get her. Since she couldn't see how far she had fallen, she didn't realize that the robbers had no way of reaching her. As her senses adjusted to the situation, she started wondering if wild animal life such as coyotes and mountain lions, could attack her. When one is pinned inside a vehicle that has gone over the side of a roadway which is leaking gasoline with no conscious companion, one's mind doesn't think clearly.

What should she do? Hazel was a survivor and had a strong will to live. She tried to convince herself there was a way out if only she could keep her wits about her. What could she do? She didn't hear any rescuers from above. No one was calling to see if they were all right. Hazel then became aware how quiet it had become. She could hear herself breathing heavily. She realized she was on her own. If she was going to get out alive it would be because of her will and determination to survive.

CHAPTER 53 THANK GOD FOR CELLPHONES

It was totally dark inside the car and she was having difficulty figuring out where she was in the car. After feeling around, she realized that she was sitting on the driver's door. Her best guess was that the car had come to rest on the driver's side. She noticed that her blouse was soaked with some type of liquid which most likely was blood. She was frightened thinking the blood had come from her wounds. Although she felt light headed, she didn't think she had lost that much blood.

She noticed that Dario's body had come to rest in the backseat of the car. Could the blood come from Dario? After touching where she hurt she didn't feel any bleeding so she surmised the blood must have come from Dario's wounds. This gave her reassurance she wasn't bleeding to death. Her thoughts then turned to being rescued. It would be only minutes before rescuers would come to her aid. Surely anyone driving along Mulholland Drive would notice that a car had gone off the road and over the embankment.

She waited and waited carefully listening for any sounds of a search party to save her. There were no sounds, it was totally quiet. The silence was comforting in that the robbers weren't after her or no wild animals were ready to attack her. Nonetheless, the stillness meant no one had noticed that they had gone over the edge. Her bruises were painful and as time went by her pain level was increasing. Also, the smell of dripping gasoline was starting to overpower the air in the crushed car.

Hazel was a cellphone freak. She loved her cellphone. At times she thought of her cellphone as a companion that was always there to help her when she was in a jam. She used her hands to try to find her purse which had been tossed all over the car. Behind the seat she was able to locate her purse stuck under a seat. She pulled the handle of the purse and when she opened it she was surprised that her cellphone was still in her purse.

She knew that the purse with the cell phone inside had hit against the car window and it was mostly likely damaged. She immediately pushed the button and the cellphone responded. By being so far down in the the ravine it was unlikely the phone would be in range of a cellphone tower. But who should she call on her cellphone for help; her parents, her neighbors, or someone from work? She had their entire phone numbers pre-programed into her phone. Or, should she attempt to call the police by dialing 9-1-1?

She was lying on her side pinned in the Jeep Cherokee. She wished there was some type of lighting so she could see how to dial 9-1-1. There was no flashlight and no car lighting. How could she dial the number? At that moment in time, Hazel reached deep down inside her survival instincts to comprehend what needed to be done. She knew her cellphone so well by memory she pressed down in the lower right-hand corner for the "9" and moved her finger up to the top number to the left which was "1" and pressed it twice.

Hazel lifted the phone up to her ear and waited and waited for a connection sound. After a delay of some time, she heard what sounded like a dispatcher. The person asked her for the purpose of her emergency. She couldn't believe that the cellphone was actually working. Her response to the dispatcher was that she was in an auto accident and was stranded in a car that had gone over a cliff.

Hazel was ecstatic that her cellphone worked and she was able to call and get through to a 9-1-1 operator. Hazel had been through a brazen attempted robbery; car crashing over an embankment; and being pinned in a car at the bottom of a ravine; and Dario wasn't moving, Hazel was in a weird state of euphoria.

The dispatcher, in a matter of fact manner, asked Hazel, "What's your location?" Hazel was taken back. She couldn't think of where she was and expected the dispatcher to do some magic to ascertain where she was. The best she could think of was that she was somewhere in the Hollywood Hills. The dispatcher was becoming skeptical whether this was a true emergency since Hazel continued to give only a vague description. She couldn't give an address or even a street because she wasn't driving and didn't know the area. Hazel possibly didn't feel comfortable telling the dispatcher that they were up on 'Lovers Lane' when they were being robbed.

The dispatchers had other calls coming in that needed attention. The dispatcher finally stated, "Ma'am if you can't tell me where you are located there is no way I can send a unit to help you." She became silent thinking of the logic of what the dispatcher had told her. Hazel didn't know how to respond. The next thing she heard was the dispatcher saying, "I'm sorry, without a location I can't help you." Hazel then heard a click and a long dial tone.

Hazel wanted to cry but she was too scared for her eyes to make tears. She sniffled and did another assessment of her situation. She tugged on the door handles and nothing moved as the doors were jammed shut. The odor of the gasoline was becoming stronger. She started to imagine that the battery might arc and set off a spark that could cause the car to ignite. If there was a fire, she would be cremated and no one would be able to identify her ashes.

CHAPTER 54 A LUCKY SAVE

All this negative thinking wasn't solving her problem. She realized that she had to think up a way to explain where she was. She remembered Dario mentioning that he was taking Beverly Glen up to the top of the hill. As they were driving eastbound on the top of the Hollywood Hills, she remembered Dario telling her that was the place where the movie stars lived on what she believed he said was Mulholland Drive. She never saw any street sign indicating the name of the street they were on.

Hazel was so frightened but she realized her only chance for survival was to see if she could convince a dispatcher who would work with her as to finding out her location. She picked up her cellphone and tried very hard to figure out from memory how to dial 9-1-1. Her cellphone was ringing and she was hoping that her cellphone battery wouldn't die on her. Finally, a male dispatcher answered and asked, "What is your emergency?" This time she put her heart and soul into the call. Strange things go through a person's mind in a stressful situation. Hazel may have been thinking of the lyrics of the Spice Girls big hit that year ***Say You'll Be There***. The other tune that hit home was LeAnn Rimes ***How Do I Live***. That would be a moot point if she couldn't persuade the dispatcher to help her out.

This time when the dispatcher said what was her location Hazel was ready to respond. She said she thought she went up Beverly Glen and they turned right and she thinks it could be Mulholland Drive. The dispatcher explained that Mulholland Drive was many miles long so could she be a little more precise. She wanted to shriek since she was doing her best with the description. The dispatcher sensed her desperation and tried to make suggestions to her so she could provide a clue where she might be.

The new dispatcher was convinced that Hazel was being truthful and needed assistance urgently. He said that he was going to request the assistance of an air ship (meaning a helicopter). Hazel could hear the dispatcher talking to the helicopter pilot and directing him to start at Beverly Glen and travel eastbound over Mulholland Drive. The spotter on the helicopter was directing the search light deep down in the canyons as they slowly moved east.

The pilot seemed a little nervous in making so much noise while beaming a bright light on so many homes of celebrities. There was fear that the pilot might get called into the captain's office to explain why several movie stars were complaining about the police helicopter disturbing their neighborhood when they were trying to sleep.

The helicopter traveled all the way to Coldwater Canyon and the spotter saw no evidence of any car over the embankments. The dispatcher was trying to think up things Hazel could do to attract the attention of the helicopter. What about turning on the lights of the car? Upon hearing that, Hazel reached around on the dashboard to try to find the headlight switch. She couldn't find the switch and she hoped that

Dario would soon wake up since he was more familiar with the Jeep. She told the dispatcher she couldn't find the light switch. Immediately the dispatcher replied by saying, honk the horn. Hazel thought why didn't she think of that? She was partly straddling the steering wheel so she pressed with all her strength on the center of the steering wheel. No response. Whatever she did the horn didn't sound. She reported to the dispatcher that nothing seemed to be working.

The pilot told the dispatcher that they would have to call a halt to the early morning search since if they continued there would be feathers ruffled at city hall. The dispatcher got back on the line with Hazel and told her that the air ship couldn't continue any longer. When Hazel heard that they were discontinuing the search she felt a crushing feeling that her life was coming to an end.

Hazel wanted to crawl up into a ball and just die. The pilot headed back to the LAPD heliport downtown. As he was approaching Laurel Canyon the spotter had turned off the light as they started speeding downtown. All of a sudden Hazel could hear the sound of a helicopter overhead and yelled at the dispatcher that she could hear the helicopter. The dispatcher got back on the frequency to the helicopter and told them the victim could hear them. The spotter turned on the bright light and shined it over the canyons. The pilot turned the helicopter back to Coldwater Canyon.

Hazel screamed at the dispatcher that she couldn't hear it any more. She said it was very faint. The dispatcher relayed that to the pilot who did a 180 with the helicopter as they proceeded back along Mulholland Drive slowly approaching to Laurel Canyon. Hazel's ears were peeled to hear any sounds from above. Then she shouted, "I can hear them, I can hear them. The spotter swung the spotlight down into a deep ravine. The pilot tried to stay in a fixed position as the spotter focused the light over some tall brush near the bottom of the ravine.

Hazel roared at the dispatcher that she could see the light from the helicopter. This was related to the pilot and the spotter. The pilot dropped altitude slightly, so the spotter could adjust the light. The spotter shouted out that he could see a reflection from a car window next to an overhanging tree. He said over the radio, "I can see what looks like a black Jeep stuck next to a tree."

The dispatcher told Hazel that he had just sent police units to respond and notified LAFD to send paramedics and a rescue team. Hazel didn't know what to say, she was truly speechless. She slowly covered her face with her hands and started to cry with joy that she would be saved.

The long ordeal was coming to an end. It seemed like it took forever for the rescuers to repel down to her. At first they wanted to make sure the car didn't continue to roll down the hill. She could feel them attach cables to the Jeep. That was followed by fire department personnel breaking some windows to get to Hazel. One paramedic went over to Dario and he checked for a pulse. The paramedic didn't say a word but turned to her and pulled her out through one of the doors that had been forcefully pried open. She was carefully placed into a rescue basket and strapped in. Hazel was having intense back pain but her head was in exhilaration as the fire department winch started to pull her up out of the ravine. Hazel, being strapped in, couldn't see how deep the ravine was. With her eyes closed she could hear the sound of the fire department wench trying to pull her inch by inch up the hill. It seemed to take a lifetime to reach the top where an ambulance was waiting to take her to the hospital. As soon as the paramedic slammed the rear door, the ambulance jerked forward. Then she could hear the sound of the siren blaring as they careened down the windy road to the hospital.

In the emergency room they tended to her injuries. No one told her how Dario was doing. She knew that he had bled a lot but she thought that he was knocked out and was unconscious from hitting his head. When she was visited by two homicide detectives she learned that her good friend Dario hadn't survived. They mentioned that they would have to wait for an autopsy to determine if he died from a bullet wound to his head or from injuries suffered from the fall over the embankment.

Hazel had mixed emotions since she was sad for the death of Dario. She had a strong romantic attachment to him and had hoped of a possible future. Nevertheless, she felt she was the luckiest person alive. She was thankful her injuries weren't life threatening. But most of all she thought how fortunate she was that she was able to use her cellphone; she finally got a dispatcher who didn't give up on her; and a pilot and spotter who went out of their way to find her in the ravine. She was so grateful to all the rescuers who risked their lives to get h

er safely out of that canyon. HAZEL FELT A STRONG INDEBTEDNESS TO SO MANY.

CHAPTER 55 BREAK IN CASE

The homicide detectives had Hazel work with a forensic artist to come up with a composite of the gunman. They had it shown on TV in hopes that someone would recognize the gunman. At first there were no leads or names and the detectives were disappointed. Then the detectives received a call several months later from an unidentified woman who provided the monikers for the gangster members who may have been involved in the Mulholland robbery/murder. The police entered the monikers through their gang computer data bank and came up with the names of Glynn Ward, Remi King, and juvenile gangsters from the Five Deuce Broadway Crips gang.

In order to see if Hazel could identify any of the possible suspects, Detective Jerry Stephens prepared a six pack photo identification line-up for suspect, Glynn Ward. On January 14, 1998, the detectives had Hazel look at the photo line-up and she had no difficulty identifying #4 as the person with the gun. She was certain he was the man who walked in front of the car and pulled out a gun from his waistband. That was the photo of Glynn Ward.

Although Hazel claimed she was certain that #4, Ward, was the gunman the detectives knew that they could never get a conviction with merely her identification. Any defense attorney could create some doubt by bringing out the fact that Hazel saw the suspect for less than a minute. That her view of the suspect was at night through tinted windows without any lighting on the suspect.

The detectives needed more evidence before they could submit the matter to the DA for any type of filing of charges. Detective Stephens went out and arrested both suspects, Glen Ward and Remi King. Since both were active gang members, the detectives weren't expecting too much in the way of cooperation. The detectives decided to see if they could get the suspects to make some type of incriminating comments when they were placed together in the backseat of a police car without any officers. The detectives gave some excuse why they had to leave the two alone. What the suspects didn't notice was the detectives had turned on a tape recorder in the front seat.

The two suspects were silent for a few minutes then they couldn't help but start talking to each other. First, they both agreed that they would pretend that they didn't know anything because they were asleep. Then Ward told Remi that someone must have informed on them. Ward said that the police didn't have any evidence on them, "unless the dude snitched about the gun." Ward said, "There is no way they can get fingerprints off that truck because ...it was dented on the driver's side..." Further, Ward made the statement that if it was about the Hollywood shooting they would have taken them to Hollywood station. The detectives had taken the suspects downtown to Parker Center and not to the Hollywood station since the case had been assigned to the Robbery Homicide Division. The suspects' misunderstanding was going to incriminate them.

The detectives then removed both suspects and took them into Parker Center and placed them in secure interview rooms. Both suspects were read their Miranda Rights and both agreed to waive them and talk. One detective spoke to Remi King first and he totally denied having anything to do with the robbery murder. After an hour and half, the detectives went to the other interview room and talked to Glynn Ward.

When they started talking to Ward, he admitted being there but it was an accident. He went on to say he didn't intend to shoot the victim. After he confessed, the detectives took him into the interview room with Remi. The detective indicated to Remi that Ward had confessed and stated, "You were the driver." This was confirmed by Ward and he was removed from that interview room.

Then Detective Stephens sat down with Remi and asked if he wanted to tell his side of what happened. Remi started from the beginning saying the three gang members went to Hollywood to look for some "prey" (someone to rob). After driving around for several hours they couldn't find any easy "prey" so they were disappointed. Then they saw a car with an attractive woman in it and they started to follow it. The cars proceeded up to Mulholland Drive and with all the twist and turns, they lost sight of the car.

As they were driving along Mulholland Drive it was quite desolate without anyone to rob. As they pulled by a car, Ward told him to stop the car. He turned off the headlights and made a U-turn and pulled up behind a Jeep. When he stopped, Ward and T-Bone got out of the car and approached the Jeep. Remi said he made another U-turn and a short time later Ward and T-Bone came running back to the car and jumped in. Later Ward told him, "look man, don't even worry about it because it wasn't supposed to happen like that. Man, if they would have just listened."

After Detective Stephens was finished with Remi, he talked to Ward again. Ward tried to explain it wasn't his fault since he didn't intend to shoot anyone. He only wanted to scare them so they didn't think he had a BB gun. Ward said the following:

"And, you know, when you barely touch it, you know, so the thing clicks—and I don't know what—my intention – I'm not no murderer."

"I don't just go say, I'm kill me somebody today."

"But it happened that way."

CHAPTER 56 DUDE, "REMEMBER THE FELONY MURDER RULE"

The detectives wrote up their reports and took the case to the DA's Office and a complaint was issued for one count of Murder, a count of Attempted Murder on Hazel, and two counts for Attempted Robberies. This would seem to be an easy case to prosecute since both Ward and Remi had admitted to being present. Defendant Ward admitted to pulling the trigger of the gun which killed Dario. He wanted to claim that he accidentally fired the gun.

However, in California as well as most states, there is what is called the **Felony Murder Rule** which consists of the following elements:

An unlawful killing

Can be: Intentional, Unintentional, or Accidental

Killing occurs during a felony,

Perpetrator had specific intent to commit a felony.

In Defendant Ward's case, it was easy to prove the unlawful killing of Dario . Defendant Ward can say that he didn't intend to kill Dario but that doesn't matter. His argument could be that all he was trying to do was scare the victim. But that doesn't matter whether the shooting was intentional or unintentional. Also, he can try to claim that he was merely tapping the gun on the driver's window and the gun went off accidentally. Still that doesn't matter, even if it was an accident.

The last issue is whether the defendant had the specific intent to commit a felony. That issue is easily proved by the prosecutor since both told the detectives that they were out looking for 'prey' which to them meant to find someone to rob.

However, the second issue became the point raised by the Defense and that was could the prosecutor prove that the KILLING OCCURRED DURING A FELONY. In this case, the Felony involved was Robbery. The elements of Robbery are as follows:

The Victim had possession of property,

The Property was taken,

Against the victim's will,

By force or fear, and

With the specific intent to permanently deprive the victim of that property.

The defendants did not commit a robbery since they didn't take any property. However, it could be an Attempted Robbery which is still a Felony within the Felony Murder Rule. But the Defense raised the issue that the Attempted Robbery was a Continuous Transaction until the defendants had reached a place of temporary safety when they reached the get-a-way car and the Felony ended at that point. (The legal argument is that one is responsible for the death of anyone killed while one is committing a Felony, as in this case, Robbery. In this case, the argument was that the Felony had ended when the robbers got back in their car, which was prior to Dario's death.)

The prosecution had to present to the jury evidence that showed that all suspects purposely went to Hollywood to rob someone. They spotted a car parked along Mulholland Drive in a desolate area where there were no other cars or people. They pulled over and made a U-turn and drove back and made another U-turn with the car's lights off. Then they pulled up behind the car. Two of them got out and tried to see if there were occupants in the vehicle. Then the one pulled a gun and approached the driver's door and announced that it was a robbery.

The fact that the victim started the engine and placed the Jeep in gear didn't interrupt the intent of the defendants to commit a robbery. Even if the driving away made it impossible for them to complete the robbery, they had the requisite intent to commit the robbery and they had acted beyond mere preparation.

Both defendants' cases were handled separately. Defendant Glynn Ward was convicted of first degree Murder as well as Attempted Robbery. This resulted in him being sentenced to Life, Without the Possibility of Parole. Defendant Ward would never have been convicted if he had understood the Felony Murder Rule and not admitted to trying to commit a Robbery and somehow the gun went off. Whether the shooting was accidental or unintentional doesn't matter.

As to Remi King, he wanted to claim he didn't know what Ward and T-Bone were going to do. He even claimed he didn't know that Ward had taken his gun from the car. However, what convicted him was the fact he told the police he was looking for 'prey' and he admitted looking for someone to rob. He couldn't claim lack of knowledge of what was about to happen when he make the U-turns to come behind the car with the car's lights off.

Remi claimed he didn't have any intentions of shooting anyone and for the fact he didn't point a gun or shoot a gun at anyone. He was merely the 'wheelman' and his involvement at most was that of an Aider and Abetter. On appeal, he claimed it was unfair for him to be treated as a murderer. The appellate court agreed with him in that they reversed his conviction for count 2, the Attempted Murder of Hazel. Although this may have seemed a hollow victory for him since they affirmed his conviction for first degree Murder and the two counts of Attempted Robbery. The bottom line was that his sentence didn't change, he still received a LWOP sentence.

We can look at the Ward and Remi cases and wonder what is wrong with this picture. Why would these gangsters want to roam outside their gang territory in order to 'prey' on law abiding victims? When these gangsters talked to the detectives they showed no conscience as to robbing people. They made it seem a standard form of behavior. In their rival gang territories it was accepted practice. However, roaming the Hollywood area for 'prey' may be where these gangsters met their downfall.

Glynn Ward was a very young man who most likely will spend 50 years behind bars. What a sad waste of a life. Ward's involvement in gangs and his criminal activities lead him to spend the next half a century behind bars.

Remi King was slightly older and will likely spend 45 years in prison. Again, a young life misguided through his involvement in gangs. The road he traveled ended up in State Prison.

Dario was a hardworking armored guard employee whose dreams will never come true.

Hazel's life almost ended on that terrifying night. The events of that evening are deeply embedded in her mind. The nightmares, anxiety, and fear will forever be with her for the rest of her life.

The following graphic page depicts the facts of this unfortunate case.

Graphics 4

LOVER'S LANE
Robbery/Murder

October 17,1997

Enjoying view parked on Mulholland Drive

Dario's Jeep Cherokee

Hazel pulled
from wreckage

Defendant Glynn Ward
Pulled Trigger

CHAPTER 57 THE REAL MULHOLLAND DRIVE

The Mulholland Drive legend continues to live. Every day and night many people traverse this famous highway. What makes it so appealing is the incredible scenic views that many would die for. The irony is on the Westside of Mulholland the Attempted Robbery and Murder of Ennis Cosby occurred during the early morning hours while nine months later, on the Eastside of Mulholland, another Attempted Robbery ended in the death of Dario . How could such a road produce such sadness while at the same time it is toasted as the 'Road to the Home of the Stars?'

Has our review of the dark side of the road taught us some lessons? In the Ennis Cosby incident, Stephanie Crain was faced with a robber with a gun and she slipped her car into Drive and accelerated out of the area. She wasn't shot or injured and lived to tell her story. However, Dario was faced with a similar situation and he started his engine and slipped the car into Drive and accelerated out of the terrifying situation he found himself in. In his case, the robber fired the gun and he was fatally shot in the head.

In everyone's life one is confronted with similar situations in which we have to make life and death decisions. We like to believe we can learn from situations that happen to others in helping us make the right choice when faced with a similar situation. If you were trying to give sage advice to a loved one, what would it be? We like to say that a person should comply with the criminal's demands if he is using a gun. The catch phrase is that your purse or wallet isn't worth dying for.

However, another point of astute advice is to quickly leave if one feels a crime is about to occur. Dario had properly assessed the situation and he had an open road ahead of him. Unfortunately, Dario miscalculated by a fraction of a second. Everyone can give Dario their 'second guessing' as to what he should have done. Most people would approach those types of situations by saying that one must be vigilant not to find oneself in a vulnerable situation. That may be why so many parents discourage their young people from going to the local Lovers Lane. From the beginning of time, young people have wanted to be alone away from adults. The hills near any urban area have always provided an enjoyable environment with a degree of solitude.

By definition, a Lover's Lane is an isolated dark place where no one will bother a couple who may want some privacy. Likewise, a robber is looking for a similar location that is isolated where he or she can commit a crime without any interference from others. Dario was a 26 year old adult who was knowledgeable about criminality since he worked for an armored truck company. His love for spectacular views of the city lights caused him to miscalculate the danger of visiting the Lover's Lane on Mulholland Drive in the Hollywood Hills.

As we have seen, Mulholland Drive is more than a Lover's Lane, but the road to the homes of many celebrities. They enjoy the privacy of living on top of the hills but they aren't immune to crime. Ennis Cosby just wanted to find a safe place to change a flat tire when he pulled off on Skirball Drive just below Mulholland Drive. Markhasev recognized that this isolated area was an excellent place to pull off a robbery since there wasn't anyone around.

Likewise, Roman Polanski realized that Jack Nicholson's place on the top of Mulholland Drive would afford him the seclusion necessary to take advantage of a 13 year old girl. There were no adults around who could step in and protect the young girl from Polanski's lascivious demands. He was obviously used to the 'Casting Couch' with all its entitlements.

Why do certain roads or highways become so famous and recognizable by the public? For one, few highways have movies named after them. Even though the movie was titled 'Mulholland Drive', it had little to do with the road itself. Mulholland Drive acquires its' notoriety really from the number of movie stars and entertainment personalities who call this street their home address. Visitors who come long distances to see firsthand what is so special about this road are generally disappointed. As one travels this highway, one isn't overly impressed by all the twists and turns you find on an asphalt country road. Most of the journey along its route reveals less than spectacular scenery.

Not until the curtain of the night falls does this famous highway reveal the magic of the city lights which creates a fascinating sight. The tapestry of twinkling lights act like magnets attracting visitors to the hypnotic splendor which is MULHOLLAND DRIVE.

Made in United States
Orlando, FL
04 November 2026

90205458R00178